" OuR life is but A VAPOR.
We ARe iN this woRld exactly like
the little sɬeAM that hovers
foR AN iNstANt oveR the cookiNg
pot. It fAdes AwAy ANd the
decisioNs foR etcRNity weRe MAde
iN its fRAgile bReath.
    The stoRy of ThoMAs Welch is
A MessAge of God showiNg At
his left hANd the fiNAl coNsequeNces
iN A lAke of fiRe, ANd iN his
Right hANd eteRNAl life iN the
poweR of Jesus ChRist.
    It is A book that will cAll foRth
fRoM its ReAdeR fAith ANd puRpose."

                        Laurel Lee

Author of the bestsellers
Walking Through the Fire
and *Signs of Spring*

$\mathcal{T}$OUCHED
by a
MIRACLE

JERRY PARRICK

Bridge-Logos *Publishers*

North Brunswick, NJ

*All Scripture references are taken from
the **King James Version** of the Bible.*

Touched by a Miracle
Copyright © 1981
by Jerry Parrick

Second Edition 1997
Library of Congress Catalog Card Number: 97-73693
International Standard Book Number: 0-88270-746-9

Bridge-Logos *Publishers*
North Brunswick Corporate Center
1300 Airport Road, Suite E
North Brunswick, NJ 08902

Contents

Foreword

Will there be a restoration of God's mighty power before Jesus comes back again?

After hearing Thomas Welch's dramatic testimony of being raised from the dead, there seems no question that God will restore all things.

In the midst of world chaos and confusion, the Holy Spirit speaks unmistakably to His chosen ones, "Fear not, for I am with you. . . . Be not afraid, for I will never leave you nor forsake you," and our voices can echo the words of the Psalmist when he wrote, "Even though I walk through the valley of the shadow of death. . . Thou art with me."

As war clouds gather on the horizon, as a new and great economic depression confronts Western civilization, as a seeming flood of evil seeks to engulf our way of life, those who know the Lord can take courage knowing that God will never leave them nor forsake them.

I have interviewed Thomas Welch on two occasions on television and have known those who have known him for many years. I feel that his experience is profound and genuine. It is the type of thing that will build faith and hope in the God of Abraham, Isaac and Jacob. As Jesus said, He *is* the God of the living and not the dead, for all live unto Him.

Pat Robertson
President,
The Christian Broadcasting Network, Inc.

Preface

You may think I've longed my whole life to bring such a momentous story to these pages. I wish I could claim such righteous cause. I can't.

When it comes to Christianity, I have closeted my schizophrenic dysfunctions of cynicism and embarrassment. I could not bear to know that mighty corporate friends might whisper charges of Pentecostal leprosy behind the backs of their hands—"Haven't you heard, he's got religion, he's now a born-again Christian"—without my being there to defend myself, "I'm one of you, I'm an Episcopalian."

On the other hand, cynicism can be ingrained and nurtured over the years and enjoyed, eventually blending with objectivity, like mixing yellow and blue on the artist's palette, never to be separated again.

The path of my feet on this planet created and shaped my dysfunctions. I landed on Normandy. I raced across France with General Patton's panzers, at the stinging tail of the strike force column, with the big howitzers. We killed men because they wore different uniforms, and they killed us.

I worked on a newspaper, a nest of cynicism in every community. I went to the University of Missouri School of Journalism, wherein the first day in 1946, Dean Mott's welcoming remarks were interrupted by a carefully orchestrated drama, with people and shots bursting on the scene. Our ensuing recorded stories were as varied as the number of eager students in the crowded hall. Journalism lesson for life: dig deep to get the true story, because people don't see and hear what they think they see and hear.

I spent many years in gray and blue suits of corporate life. At the bottom rung, where I knew as much of grand strategy as I did when Patton was leading us in Europe— nothing. Then the middle rungs, and then those near the top.

Where credentials of prestigious eastern universities and country clubs and elitist scholastic disciplines and executive cloning and "perks" were intertwined with pecking order, bloody power struggles on the executive floor, inside "CIA" surveillance and operations, territorialism, towering egos, cliques, vendettas, white male domination and interlocking boards of directors networking the power base among banking, oil, steel, insurance, manufacturing, utilities, real estate and politics. Producing hordes of trapped corporatecrats, eventually drained of initiative, objectivity, freedom, personality and even protest, lest the supreme goals and rewards—promotions, pay raises and retirement security—be withdrawn by their captains of corporate power.

Out of all this I met Thomas Welch, whose hands were as clean as mine were unclean. Who knew nothing about the supersophistication, humble arrogance and unerring benevolence of the corporate man and yet who knew everything, because of something that happened on the way to his becoming what some might call him later, Saint Thomas.

When I learned of the miracle, called by Gordon Lindsay "one of the greatest miracles of the twentieth century," and Thomas Welch's subsequent exemplary life of Christian service, I knew I had to crawl inside his psyche and look at his role in this incredible story, being chosen by God to bring a message to the world.

At one point during the long hours of interviewing, taping and writing, I mentioned the manuscript was moving with all the speed of a snail. Reverend Welch leaned back in his living room chair, chuckled and, with a twinkle in his eye, said, "Jerry, it all takes time and patience. You know, God is one of the slowest men you'll ever meet."

Not long after, I was sitting at the typewriter in my study, still impatient with my progress, when I heard a voice inside suddenly tell me, "Read Isaiah 30, verse 8." I didn't even know if there was an Isaiah 30, verse 8. I protested, feeling it was probably some more painful pruning that was going on at the time. I was so exhausted, I was really ready to give up the project entirely. I reached for my Bible, leafed to the passage, and with eyes that smiled wider with every word, I read, "Now go, write it before them in a table, and note it in a book, that it may be for the time to come for ever and ever."

Toward the end of our meetings on the book, I told Reverend Welch, "With all the crosswinds of Christian doctrine, it's going to take courage to joust with some of those who will read this book and disagree with you and perhaps attack you openly."

Without hesitating, Reverend Welch replied, "This has come up many times. My response has always been straightforward: God wrought the miracle on Larch Mountain. I was given no choice; I was chosen to play a role in that miracle. Who am I to question what God does? Who am I to try to yoke what God creates with man's doctrine? Of this I am certain because I was there: the miracle came from Almighty God himself. He gave me a message to take to the world, and I have done that, as faithfully as I know how."

Jerry Parrick

Introduction

Few men die twice. Few men experience a deadly fall and have it turn into a miraculous encounter with eternity. Few men are touched by a miracle . . . wherein an Almighty glance bestows the pinnacle of the miracle: "Return to life." That is why I am telling this to you. I've said "few men" – it could be women – but I said "men" because it happened to my grandfather, Thomas Welch. My grandfather was in the presence of the Lord. The miracle goes on. You are not alone.

At eighteen, my grandfather fell and then experienced a miraculous encounter with eternity. My grandfather was touched by a miracle. My grandfather was in the presence of the Lord. The miracle goes on. You are not alone. I have been touched by that miracle, and countless others around the world have heard, read, and have also been touched by that miracle.

For fifty years my grandfather told about the overwhelming holy assurance, amazing grace, fulfilled faith, and inspiring charisma emanating from that miracle. He told it to countless families, parents, audiences, on national and regional television, radio news media and in this book. All this, all this before I then said: My grandfather has now died twice." The miracle goes on. You are not alone.

I have been given the mantle to tell you, to tell the world, about the most inspiring, most uplifting, blessed by faith . . . my grandfather's miraculous encounter with eternity. I have been joined by my lovely wife, Kay Silva, to spread the warmth of faith emanating exponentially out, and forever, as concentric circles from the dynamic center of that miracle.

My formative years were spent with my grandfather. In my first seven years I was raised in his home, a home of love, of learning, of praise, of faith, with both grandparents, my mother, brother and sister. In the Welch family I watched and grew as they poured out their lives into the fulfillment of their commitments to God. The Lord led Thomas and Gretta Welch together. She played the organ and sang. All the while he led his ministry through the years in a divine testimony of faith about the miracle on Larch Mountain and his resurrection.

As the Lord led Thomas and Gretta Welch, the Lord has led Jeff and Kay Edwards. Kay is a recording artist, song writer, and performer of Country Gospel music. We share a common interest. We devote our lives to God. Our prophetic song ministry, traveling and performing, gives us joy together, as we serve the Lord and spread the meaning of the miracle in our grandfather's life together, in God's love and in His Holy Spirit.

The ministries of Reverend's Welch, Lindsay and Hall demonstrated that the Lord will spread His spirit throughout the world. Today we grow in the spirit through their prophetic words. The growing world of people who have listened and have been touched by the miracle have stepped forward to have their lives blessed by the Kingdom of God. This is our ministry:

*Walking in the Spirit of the Lord today to give the glory and praise to God,

* Sharing a prophetic song ministry with my wonderful wife, Kay Silva Edwards,

* Continuing our grandfather's fifty-year ministry leading others to the Lord.

We just want you to know . . . as we have learned from our grandfather's trip to hell and back: God has a plan for each of our lives. The miracle goes on. You are not alone. You too can be touched by the miracle.

Jeff Welch-Edwards

1
Violent Death

This turned out to be the kind of a day engraved on tombstones. I died this day.

Nonetheless, no man ever chiseled this day in stone for me. I was never buried.

Eyewitnesses crowd around my corpse in a room heavy with shock. These men saw me fall to a violent death. They probed the bottom of a mountain pond desperately in an almost unyielding search for my body.

They watch my cold cadaver in silence, suddenly stunned by what they think they see, a soft, faint movement in my eyelids.

All eyes shoot open and lock on me in grim awe. Yes! Yes! They moved! They moved!

Tears slowly form in the corners of my eyes, hesitate for an instant, then course down my temples.

Deep within me, the stilled, stagnant force of life begins to cascade anew. My body stirs. In a few moments I open my eyes. I look up into a sea of faces.

They are witnessing more than an extraordinary,

1

incredible chain of events. They are seeing an amazing miracle.

The miracle began to unfold as I was killed in a fall into a mountain pond. I was dead for an hour, most of that time under ten feet of water. I journeyed to a burning, turbulent, rolling ocean of fire in the next world. And I was returned to life on earth by a divine resurrection.

The day opened quite differently, at the cool, blue end of the danger spectrum. An important job had recently been offered to me. Looking forward with eager anticipation to this day, it finally arrives.

This is my first day of work as a fledgling engineer at a logging mill on Larch Mountain, pretty heady stuff for a lad of eighteen.

My primary responsibility encompasses the operation of a powerful steam engine located high on the top deck of a trestle that stands as tall as a five-story building.

The morning hums along, exciting for me, but uneventful for the mill. After lunch, close to one-thirty, a heavy overcast threatens rain.

Near my work area on the trestle's top deck, a huge log sixty feet long is being slabbed on a holding carriage, sawed into four sides, two feet by four feet.

The sawyer engages chain hooks to pull the mammoth timber onto a conveyor that is supposed to take it out to a flume, a large water-filled trough, for a four-mile trip down the mountain to the next sawmill on the mighty Columbia River.

But the timber jams on a conveyor guard before it reaches the flume.

I grab a pole with a pick on the end and run out to dislodge it. If I can just unwedge the giant, the conveyor will drop it in the flume. I look around. No one shows up to help me.

I sink my pickaroon into the timber and shake it. As I sway it back and forth, I feel I'm just about to pull it free.

I pull as hard as I can. The hook slips. My own force throws me headlong off the top of the trestle.

I'm falling five stories to a violent death.

2
Calm Before the Storm

I was quite unprepared to be chosen for a miracle at the age of eighteen.

I don't mean to imply that anyone is ever "prepared" for a miracle, in the same sense an astronaut might be tutored in esoteric knowledge for a trip to a distant planet.

However, I was a very unlikely candidate. I had made no commitment to be a Christian. I had not attended church regularly. I was not contemplating a Christian life.

In fact, because of what had happened earlier in my life, I was still mad at God the day I fell into the pond at the logging mill on Larch Mountain.

I'll never forget my curiosity, prompting me for the first time to ask my mother, "Where is God, mommy?" I was six.

She took me by the hand, led me out of our home into the night, pointed up to a bright, starry sky and said with love in her soft voice, "I'm not sure exactly where, Tommy, but God is up there. And, Tommy, remember, He'll always be watching everything you do."

"Up there" was a nice place to live as far as I was concerned. Only a year ago the tail of Halley's comet had sprinkled angel dust across the evening heavens among the stars. What a beautiful, shimmering afterglow.

To me her answer was moving and profound. I looked up at the splendor of that panorama of twinkling stars, and I couldn't see God either, but now I knew where to look when I wanted to talk to Him.

And six years later, I wanted to talk to Him.

Out from my childhood habitat sprawled wild, pioneer country on the plains of Alberta, just east of the majestic Canadian Rocky Mountains.

I was born on our old homestead on Miquelon Lake, the first of four children, on October 24, 1905, to Peter Marvin Welsh and Julia Nomeland Welsh. My forebears were Norwegian, Irish, Austrian and German.

At one time the family name was spelled Welsche. That must have disturbed someone, because my parents inherited Welsh, which was entered on my birth certificate. I was not comfortable with the "s" so I changed my own name later to Welch.

Within a year my father purchased a ranch of three hundred and twenty acres, close to Kingman and not far from Edmonton. Harry, May and Pearl were born here, all of us about two years apart.

Everyone in our family of six lived a warm, happy, uncomplicated life. Our father and mother were a handsome couple. They were very close and loved each other deeply—just how deeply I would soon learn not long after turning eleven.

None of us ever heard them quarrel. Maybe they did, but we never heard them.

As was the rest of the community, we were hard-working, law-abiding Canadians, with high regard for the rights of other people. There was a tranquility in our home, which was a heritage of our family's belief in God and traditional values.

We had symbols that embodied our principles and our values. They were more than a building, a landscape, a person or some other form. They were as dynamic as life itself.

Like the church in Kingman. Out of a plain, white building rose a tall, white steeple with a white cross on top. Our little house of God literally glowed with worship and love and fellowship. That symbol represented a cherished dimension in all our lives.

Like the wondrous Canadian Nature. Oh, how I looked forward to my four-day safaris into that rugged landscape, alone except for three friends, my horse, my dog and my rifle. The sky formed a roof, and all of Nature's life-threatening and life-support systems might be within a hundred yards in any direction at any time.

Like the Royal Canadian Mounted Police. The officer was unique by uniform, bearing and authority. He stood out more in the inner chambers of our imagery than in real life, because he rode into town only occasionally. But we respected that symbol as compassionate, unerring and the epitome of all the virtues of law and order, backed up by appropriate artillery, a long-barreled pistol and a thirty-thirty in the scabbard.

My grandfather was a circuit-riding Lutheran minister and schoolteacher. Everyone looked forward to the day he would arrive in Kingman.

People would run out to meet him when his horse cantered into town. For the kids it meant special instruction in addition to the schooling we received within our families. And for most everyone it meant an opportunity to go to church.

Religion was a part of my family's way of life, but we were no more religious than any of the other families. We were Lutherans. We read the Bible. We attended church when there were services, and we were taught there is a spiritual tie between God and man.

We believed what Martin Luther preached, "The just shall live by faith," and that God spoke to Luther. We understood and believed God can speak to any man.

I was thoroughly enjoying life. I learned everything eagerly. I thrived in the security of our own ranch.

The love in our family bound us closely together. I worked hard on the ranch. I jumped at the chance to live in the wilderness whenever possible. I never felt I was intruding on Nature; rather, I was a part of Nature.

I shot my first timber wolf when I was seven. And I trapped ninety muskrats, which carried prime fur in great demand, on the back slough of our ranch to earn money.

But now, I was approaching eleven, and though I had no inkling of it, my world was about to collapse around me, not just a little, completely.

3
So Much to Be Sad About

It was hot. The early part of July.

My dad was a big, powerful man, not afraid of work. He was putting a grain tank on a wagon, by himself.

All of a sudden something snapped inside his head. Dad wobbled into the house, complaining he was dizzy and sick. He lay down and recovered. At least, as far as I knew.

But he must have secretly harbored the knowledge he was not well. One day dad kept an appointment with his doctor. After an examination, Dr. Norby told him, "Pete, I can't find anything wrong. However, I'll tell you what I'd recommend. I think you should give serious consideration about going back to Mayo Clinic in Rochester.

"Mayo has the latest equipment, and those doctors are specialists with advanced diagnostic techniques. They can determine if we've got a problem here. And, if we do, what should be done about it."

Dad told Dr. Norby he'd think about it. And he did. But not for long. The cost would be substantial and he reasoned he didn't have the time; he was indispensable; the harvest season was approaching.

Dad assured us, "Don't worry. I'll just take it easy for a while. I'll feel better. I know I will."

By September my father was confined to bed at home. I knew his distress. I was taking care of him. He was in great pain, nauseous, unable to maintain his balance standing up, sweating profusely and wracked with headaches. He deteriorated, lost weight and wasted away.

In early October dad's condition became so grave that Dr. Norby informed us he had concluded the strenuous lifting must have caused a blood vessel to rupture in his head, which led to a rapidly growing tumor. His prognosis left no room for hope.

Several weeks later, amid a house of gloom, dad died. He was forty-four.

In a blustery cemetery, my father was buried, through two inches of snow, on my eleventh birthday.

We were all grief-stricken. Our rudder was gone. Mother was so grief-stricken she became ill. It occupied no more than passing thought in my mind; it would only be temporary.

But Dr. Norby put her to bed, and alarmingly she became progressively worse.

I couldn't believe this. What was happening?

The loss of my father was too overwhelming to handle. I would still wake up every morning feeling I could call out to the next room, "Dad," and he would answer. But then a wave of thought would rush toward me, peak, curl and crash over me with reality, shattering my world again and again.

Now, I had to know about mother. On the doctor's next visit I motioned him aside into another room. After we settled down at the breakfast table, I asked a question I really didn't want to know the answer to, unless it was the answer I wanted to hear, "Is mother going to get well?"

As he sat before me, Dr. Norby closed his eyes. He dropped his head until his eyelids rested on the thumb and forefinger of his left hand. Dr. Norby gently closed his fingers across his eyelids until they pinched the bridge of his nose.

He responded, "Tommy," and then he looked at me over glasses he wasn't wearing, "your mother is dying of a broken heart.

"She can live if she wants to live. But she won't eat. She won't take nourishment. She simply does not want to live without your father."

Without my father?

My heart cries out what my lips can't speak, "But what about me?"

Finally, in February, death returned. Mother died.

Just four months after we had said goodbye to my father, we returned to the blustery cemetery.

My mother was buried through a foot of snow, side by side with my father.

I'm no longer a son. I'm an orphan.

Our ranch was sold. A summit meeting of relatives and friends decided I would live with Uncle Sam and Aunt Julia on their ranch, and my brother, Harry, and sisters, May and Pearl, would be dispatched to live with others.

I tried not to be a burden. I joined my uncle's family; but I really didn't yoke my life with the loving niche they opened up for me. How could I cope with all the emotions of mourning and survival amid new relationships?

I coped in the only way I knew how. I put a damper on my youthful enthusiasm. I built a wall around me. I became more and more withdrawn. I became stoical.

Even though my aunt and uncle were very kind to me, I missed my mother and father desperately. And I was separated from my brother and sisters. There was no longer any family that was *my* family.

I was dreadfully lonely.

There was something else. Every Saturday night neighbors gathered at my uncle's ranch for a country dance.

The evening would develop into a big, noisy party with lots of drinking. This revelry really repulsed me. It's not that I was not invited; I was.

But how could the world wallow in dancing and drinking and laughter and merrymaking when there was so much to be sad about?

One Saturday night I could stand it no longer. As usual a party was roaring in progress. The decibel level climbed higher and higher to an intolerable crescendo in the house and within me. The grandfather clock told the only person listening it was ten o'clock. Outside, fiercely cold weather had driven the thermometer's mercury down somewhere between forty and fifty degrees below zero.

I ran out of the house to the milk barn, where there was a separate room with a wood stove and bed. I'd slept out there often. I crumpled down on the bed.

No one loved me. I was alone, disconsolate, sorrow-stricken. Painful, forlorn feelings engulfed and terrified me. Without any question, no pain could be more excruciating than this.

A tear welled up in my eye and spilled down my cheek. I began to cry.

My anger and I roused together. I walked outside and looked up at a bright northern sky. It seemed close enough to touch. I gazed at those stars, now cold, where mother had pointed her finger.

I'm sure, God, you're up there. I close my right fist, raise it, shake it at the heavens in the face of God, and blurt between sobs, "God, I'm mad at you. I don't like you anymore. You didn't have to do this to me."

The only thing that ensues is the silence of the universe. I'm not aware of any response, let alone recognition.

In the following months I tried to become the coldest stoic of them all. I decided finally, "God, if you're up there, I'm convinced you're not going to do anything for me. What you've done already is unforgivable. You could have prevented the deaths of my father and mother. Why didn't you? Why?"

In the next year death struck close to me again. Ben Grandahl, a school chum, died of cancer of the jaw, after a long bout of illness that started with an infected tooth. Try as I might, I couldn't grow a hide callous enough to protect me from the pervasive sadness of continuing tragedy.

And death stalked the ranch. A worldwide epidemic

13

washed over our home, threatening my bedrock security once again. Influenza took a bead down its rifle barrel on the lives of my foster parents, Uncle Sam and Aunt Julia.

4
Mysterious Peg-Leg Stranger

Like runners madly passing the baton in a relay race, carriers passed a killer virus from one to another in 1918, to rush influenza to Kingman and all the way out to us at the ranch.

A deadly flu epidemic ravaged the world and swept across the expanse of our vast, frozen Canadian winter.

Whole families succumbed to the scourge. Rare was the family that didn't lose at least one member.

And tragically worse, bodies were stashed in barns and hayricks until spring, because of frozen ground. Even if a spade could have penetrated the tundralike surface, there were not enough able-bodied men to bury the dead.

Our ranch family was not immune. The disease rampaged through our midst. Raging fever and hacking cough struck down Uncle Sam and Aunt Julia. They were deathly ill, along with two of my four cousins, Hilda and Selma.

Torval, a baby of six months, seemed untouched by the flu; we kept him isolated.

Only cousin Olive and I were well enough to crawl out of bed, nurse the others, prepare meals, take care of the household and run the ranch. My nickname for Olive was "Toots"; she and I were thirteen. How we managed to avoid intensive care ourselves, after the influenza disabled so many in our family, I'll never know.

One day, after tending to our chores of feeding and watering the livestock, Toots and I were sitting down and resting by a window. We looked out across a snow-covered field toward a grove of poplar trees. On the other side of the poplars, and hidden by them from our view at the window, was Kingman.

As Toots and I talked, we noticed a man walk out of the grove of trees; he crossed through the snow, heading for our house.

The closer he got, the more clearly we discerned his distorted gait. When he walked, he rose on his left leg and swung his right leg. Soon we saw it; he had a wooden leg. Out of a knee-length right trouser, a rough-hewn two-by-four now tapered down to a peg.

Completely spellbound, Toots and I froze as we heard the stranger crunch and thump across the porch. We heard him stop, shuffle a little, then pound on the front door.

I didn't know what to do. Who was this man? Was he a thief, a murderer? We were stuck out here all alone, defenseless, utterly helpless. Uncle Sam couldn't rise to fight a shadow. And I was no match for this towering frontiersman.

I thought of my gun, but I also thought, if he's here to

do us harm, he's armed anyway; I couldn't approach the door with a gun.

I opened the door.

His commanding presence was overwhelming.

"I've come to take care of you. My name is Hogg." That's all he said.

I let him in.

He stumped into the house, looked around and made his way to the bedrooms, where misery lay writhing and hacking in bed after bed.

Out of his shirt pocket popped a thermometer. Mr. Hogg proceeded to take the temperature of each patient, meanwhile assuring Uncle Sam he was here solely to take care of us and the ranch as long as he was needed during this crisis.

After taking the temperature of those in bed, he pushed the thermometer in my mouth. As he read the results, he pursed his lips and shook his head.

"You're next. Get yourself to bed right now, and stay there. You don't have to worry about a thing. I'll take care of everyone."

Before Toots and I knew what was happening, the peg-leg stranger tucked us into bed, prepared food and fed us.

Everything Toots and I had been doing our unknown visitor now accomplished, from preparation of meals to nursing the sick ward, to around-the-house drudgery, to taking care of the livestock, to meeting the normal, routine emergencies of ranch life.

He easily dispatched a herculean work schedule.

Without any question, one thing struck me as odd.

Although the frontiersman rested and slept, none of us ever saw him mussed up, in disarray or in other clothes. He wore the same bright-colored woolen shirt and outdoor work pants. Yet, he was always clean and fresh.

One by one each of us recovered. We rejoiced we were one of the few families around that had not lost at least one member.

It was now six weeks since our mysterious peg-leg stranger had pounded on the front door.

One evening we were all sitting together at the old, solid ranch table enjoying dinner with Mr. Hogg, when he informed us, "Well, it's time for me to move on.

"You're all well now. The ranch is in fairly good shape. We haven't lost one head of livestock. And I've done what I've come to do."

Uncle Sam was suddenly moved emotionally like I'd never seen him before.

"You know, there are no words I can say that will ever repay you for what you've done.

"There's no money in this world that could ever repay you for the lives of my family."

My uncle reached into his pocket, pulled out a roll of bills and respectfully placed them in front of our guest.

"I'd like for you to take this token. It's all I have here at the present time. I know it's not enough for what you've done, but I want you to have it. Tomorrow I'll go into Kingman to draw some more from the bank, to give you before you go."

Mr. Hogg smiled and looked at each of us around the table, stopping as he gazed at my uncle, whose face expressed the genuine love we all felt for this man. His large, weathered hand reached for the roll of bills, and he peeled off only one of the notes.

He returned the remainder of the money to my uncle, after which he folded the bill and placed it in his shirt pocket, saying, "This will do."

Uncle Sam tried to insist the stranger take all the money, but he declined, "Thank you, this is all I'll need. Your family will be needing that money. You see, the only reason I'm here is because the Lord told me to come."

And that's all he would say.

The next morning Mr. Hogg rose, finished his breakfast, bid us goodbye and left. Toots and I rushed to the window and watched him walk across freshly fallen snow into the grove of poplar trees. He entered the woods and disappeared.

Immediately we noticed something was missing. As air leaves a child's balloon, gone was the glow that emanated from our benefactor and filled our home to overflowing with an incomparable warmth of love and peace.

The mysterious peg-leg stranger took the glow with him. No, there was a significant nuance of difference. He didn't *take* it with him; I didn't understand, but it seemed to me *the glow left* with him, to *accompany* him wherever he went.

An hour later Uncle Sam hitched up a horse and rode into Kingman. He withdrew additional money and went in search of Mr. Hogg. To his utter astonishment, not only did no one know a Mr. Hogg, no one had seen a man with a wooden leg.

After my uncle returned with this baffling news, several of us went to look for the stranger. We followed his tracks in the snow from our house into the woods, where they disappeared. We thought perhaps we had just lost them, so we circled the grove, but no tracks could be found coming out of the woods either.

As far as we were concerned, our mysterious guest just vanished. We didn't see him, hear from him or hear anything about him again.

One of the last things my mother had asked me on her deathbed was to promise I would study for confirmation at the Bethlehem Lutheran Church in Dinant.

I promised. And I was confirmed at the age of fourteen.

Over the next few years I wandered away from my religious ties but not from the virtuous heritage of my family. I became more of a loner. Two other loners became good friends, Harry Olsen and Gustave "Gus" Brocke, whose older brother would become important in my life very soon.

The three of us had learned to take care of ourselves. We felt pretty self-reliant. At this point we spent most of our time in school. There wasn't any dating, any romance. A loner doesn't surrender his independence to anyone, least of all a girl.

We made a pact we would live clean, wholesome lives. We three youngsters were youthfully solemn; we meant it. We shook hands on it.

Then I entered Alberta College and spent about a year in study before I decided it was time to get a permanent job. I was now eighteen.

Gus's brother, Thorfin "Fin" Brocke, pronounced "Brocky," was chief engineer at a logging mill in the United States. He and his wife, Mabel, extended an invitation for me to visit them for a few months in their home near Portland, Oregon.

My hosts were good friends from Canada. Mabel had become ill when they lived in Alberta, and Fin thought a complete change in living style and climate would be beneficial.

I soon discovered there was more than a geographical change; there was a dynamic spiritual change. They told me they had accepted Jesus Christ into their lives.

Mabel told me she was no longer ill and it had nothing to do with living in the United States. It had everything to do with a miracle.

An evangelist by the name of Everett Parrott had visited Portland. He was holding a revival in a tent at Fourteenth and South East Hawthorne.

His exhortation was emblazoned on a sign outside for all to see: "Salvation for the Soul and Healing for the Body."

The Brockes were deeply moved by the miraculous healings they saw, when those in the audience who were sick went forward for prayer.

Mabel's own illness had recently been diagnosed by her doctor. He told her she had a serious heart condition, with but a short time to live. She had guessed it was terminal, because pain had progressed to the point where it was unbearable.

Mable turned to the Bible. She believed if the Scriptures said one could be healed by Jesus, then one could. And that's exactly what her Bible told her. So Mabel informed her doctor, to his consternation, she would not continue in treatment.

During one of the revival meetings Mabel went forward for prayer. She told Reverend Parrott she had a serious heart disease, and he immediately responded by laying hands on her and praying to Jesus Christ for a healing.

Mabel told me the miracle happened right there, instantly. The pain was gone. The disease was gone. She was healed. Her doctor later went as far as medical science could allow him to go, understandably, by confirming the temporary absence of her heart condition.

Evangelist Parrott's wife, Myrtle, was the sister of a woman who would become world famous much later for her incredible healing ministry—Kathryn Kuhlman.

The Brockes went to church regularly, and I accepted their invitation on occasion to go with them. I was very impressed by what was happening in their lives. Mabel had been praying for many months that the same thing would happen in my life, too.

I listened closely to the minister of their church. Dr. John G. Lake had traveled all over the world and had been a missionary in South Africa.

He preached a message of God's love and His power to heal sickness, bondage and sin in all those who would believe. I thought the gospel preached by Dr. Lake was wonderful if it were true, but I could never bring myself to believe it was true for me.

My eyes saw, and my ears heard, all this. And I know it pained Mabel deeply that I did not go forward to ask Jesus Christ to come into my life. She wanted everyone prepared for eternity in the way of her faith without the loss of a single minute.

But I was not convinced. There was a little self-righteous tilt to my nose. I felt I had led a pretty religiouslike life. Moreover, I had a whole lifetime ahead of me.

If there were a God, I thought, surely I was as pure and good as He. I was still deeply wounded by what He had done to me, taking my father and mother. I was still angry at Him.

Fin was the chief engineer at the Bridal Veil Lumber Company sawmill on Larch Mountain. Called the Palmer Mill, it was about thirty miles east of Portland.

The company employed over one hundred and fifty men in logging and sawmill operations. The Brockes had homes in Portland and also near the mill, where I had been staying.

One night Fin told me the workload at the mill required the addition of another man. He offered me a job as a second engineer.

My smile was all the answer he needed.

5
Death in the Afternoon

Everyone finished lunch at one o'clock and returned to work.

This was my first day as an engineer at a logging mill of the Bridal Veil Lumber Company. It was Monday, June 30, 1924.

And what a day it was going to be!

The morning was exciting for me. I met fellow workers. I got acquainted with my responsibilities. For the mill, the morning was routine.

But not the afternoon. In thirty minutes the distress whistle would pierce the mountain air. An emergency of violent death would shut down the entire mill.

Located on Larch Mountain in northern Oregon, the company's Palmer sawmill was four miles above the mighty Columbia River, which flows out of Canada through the American Northwest to the Pacific Ocean.

Muscle, machinery, gravity and water fed the mill's insatiable appetite for power.

A mountain stream had been dammed up to form

several ponds. The upper pond spanned over one hundred and fifty feet from one side to the other at the widest point.

In the middle of the upper pond stood a massive trestle, as tall as a five-story building.

Rail cars hauled logs from distant points and dumped them into the lower pond. They were moved later by conveyor belt up to the top deck of the trestle for sawing on a holding carriage.

A steam engine was also on the top deck, not far from the carriage. This powerhouse was my responsibility, along with five other engines which supplied power for the whole mill, including electricity, conveyor belts, saws and machinery.

On this day we were cutting the largest logs of yellow and red fir ever cut in the mill.

The presence of danger was heavy everywhere, especially around the logs when they were being sawed and moved.

It was approaching one-thirty. Seventy men were working in and around the logging mill.

I was tending the steam plant on the top deck.

Gordon Speer sat down below in the cab of his locomotive while logs were being unloaded into the lower pond from the train. He was looking up my way.

Mabel Brocke was picking mountain dewberries by the schoolhouse on a hillside on the other side of the draw, not far from the mill.

Mabel Burness, Mabel's ten-year-old niece, was visiting from Portland to pick berries. However, at this time she was playing by the upper pond.

Julius Gunderson had just arrived after driving up from Portland. He was in the mill office talking with Fin Brocke about a job.

Jimmy Gaydon was a sawyer operating the main saw not too far away from me on the top deck.

It was now close to one-thirty. A heavy overcast threatened rain.

Near my work area on the trestle's top deck, a huge log sixty feet long was being slabbed on the holding carriage, sawed into four sides, two feet by four feet.

The sawyer engaged chain hooks to pull the mammoth timber onto a conveyor that was supposed to take it out to a flume, a large water-filled trough, for a four-mile trip down the mountain to the next sawmill on the Columbia River.

But the timber jammed on a conveyor guard before it reached the flume.

I grabbed a pole with a pick on the end and ran out to dislodge it. If I could just unwedge the giant, the conveyor would drop it in the flume. I looked around. No one had showed up to help me.

I sank my pickaroon into the timber and shook it. As I swayed it back and forth, I felt I was just about to pull it free.

I pulled as hard as I could. The hook slipped. My own force threw me headlong off the top of the trestle.

I'm falling five stories to a violent death.

I grabbed for anything I could hold onto; there was nothing.

I didn't yell. The only thought going through my mind

was that I didn't have a chance of surviving this fall.

After that, I remember nothing.

The rest of what happened was told to me later. At least, that which happened at the mill.

6
Dredging Murky Waters

I plunged headfirst from the top deck of the trestle, five stories above the pond.

I slammed into a crossbeam with the top of my head, hit the timber with my body, cartwheeled off, continued falling out of control, smashed into a lower beam, splashed into the pond and sank out of sight.

Gordon Speer leaned out of the cab of his locomotive. Horror-struck, he watched me fall, then marked the spot where I went into the water. Speer grabbed the cord, blew his train whistle in a call of emergency and ran to find Fin Brocke, who was now in the main engine room. He blurted out news of the accident.

Fin immediately shut down the operations of the entire mill. A phone call summoned an ambulance from Portland, thirty miles away.

Some of the crew used log-balancing skills to wend their way out on the narrow, low beam of the trestle to look for me in the water. The train engineer pointed to where I disappeared; the water was too murky to see anything.

Others found a skiff and joined the search.

Gunderson, who was on his first trip to the mill applying for a job, stood on the bank of the pond. He watched the men on the beam dredge for my body with pike poles.

"I'm only a visitor," he thought, reluctant to take part. "The old hands must be experienced at this sort of thing."

Gunderson remained there at least thirty minutes. He looked for air bubbles or any clue where I might be located. A few in the search party on the lower beam discontinued the search.

Gunderson made his way out on the beam.

One of the men, who had done all he could, gave me up for lost and handed his pike pole to Gunderson, who suspected the reason I hadn't been found was that I was on the bottom, ten feet below the surface.

He took the pole and probed the bottom. The pike pole had a long handle with a hook at the end, for moving logs, timbers and debris. Gunderson dredged a large area, thrusting his pole completely underwater. Still, no telltale air bubbles appeared on the surface of the water to guide him.

A feeling began to spread among the men of the dredging party. Recovery now was for the sake of my body, not my life.

Far too much time had passed. The urgency began to subside. Any possibility of finding me alive had vanished.

When suddenly, finally, the fishing end of the pole signaled Gunderson, a strike! the fish was caught!

As Gunderson describes it, "I hooked onto his clothes

and pulled his body near enough for us to get our hands on him, and we pulled him out. He was dead. There was no life in him at all. His head was smashed in on top and blood was everywhere."

Fin, Gunderson and some of the crew huddled around my lifeless form; they perched me precariously on the beam and clutched me firmly as best they could; after some forty-five minutes on the bottom of the Palmer Mill pond, this was no time for me to slip back into the water.

Spectators lined the banks of the pool and the top of the trestle; eyes were hanging on every movement, ears on every word.

Several men maneuvered the skiff close enough to transfer my body on board for a trip to the far side of the pond near the mill office.

The skiff was beached among a crowd of people. Fin examined me; I wasn't breathing. Fingers searched for my pulse; no throb, no life, nothing.

I was dead. Across my scalp the skin was ripped open. My skull revealed a fissure, the back edge smashed below the front edge, when my head slammed into the beam.

I was covered with blood. Cold mountain water drained from my skin, my hair and my clothing.

Someone sprinted to get a wire basket to transport me to the office. Rain began to pelt down upon the crowd.

Fin looked at me, shook his head, turned on his heel and dashed for home, to get Mabel. Mabel's niece ran to accompany him.

Picking berries on a hillside near the school, Mabel

Brocke felt the first few drops of the leading edge of the storm and scurried home.

As she approached the house, she saw her husband and young Mabel Burness rushing up.

Fin shouted across the way, "Mama, Tommy fell. He's dead."

Mabel blanched, stunned, puzzled. Questions flooded her mind; she selected one with great reverent meaning for her.

She cried out, "Why Tommy?"

More puzzling was what happened next. In answer to her question, according to Mabel, "I heard a voice say, 'For the glory of God.' "

It didn't make sense. She and Fin had been praying for me for many months. I had not made the commitment which was the tapestry of their prayers. And now I was dead.

How could this be for the glory of God?

Only a fiery new Christian like Mabel, whose faith was too starched to be wrinkled by doubt, could know somehow, someway, since she'd been told, this would be for the glory of God.

Fin looked down into her anguished face, "I've come to get you to pray." As they hurried to the mill office in the rain, they prayed all the way.

Some of the men lifted my body from the skiff to the wire basket. They carried the basket into the mill office, wrapped a blanket around me and placed my body on a table.

Gunderson, Speer, Gaydon, a gang-sawyer and other

members of the crew packed the office. They searched for answers almost in whispers, as if this were the family viewing room in a funeral home.

Rain poured down on the roof. Apparently, nothing more could be done for me here; the ambulance was on its way.

And so were the Brockes. Mabel and Fin approached the office and rushed into the room. Men stepped back to make way as Mabel went to my side, and Fin to the other.

They looked down at the corpse and, according to Mabel, "His face and head were covered with blood. There was no pulse, no life. Surely we were in the presence of death. You could feel it as well as see it."

Mabel's deep and powerful faith told her something more could be done for me here. Her Bible declared solemnly and she believed, "Is any sick among you? let him call for the elders of the church; and let them pray over him, anointing him with oil in the name of the Lord: And the prayer of faith shall save the sick, and the Lord shall raise him up; and if he have committed sins, they shall be forgiven him" (James 5:14-15).

Fin anointed my head with oil according to the Scripture. He looked at his wife. "Mabel, you pray."

She placed one hand in the blood on my head and the other on my heart. A young man took her hand off my head and protested to Mabel, "Can't you see that's where he's hurt?"

With blood oozing out between her fingers, Mabel persisted and prayed her short, simple supplication to spare my life and save my soul because, by her firebrand calipers, I wasn't a Christian.

"Lord," she said, "I've prayed for Tom too long, and I'm not going to let him go. You've got to send him back."

Mabel repeated the prayer over and over, in different words.

While all this was going on—the dredging, the recovery of my body from the bottom of the mountain pond and Mabel Brocke praying for me in the mill office—I wasn't on earth. At the same time, I was very much alive.

To describe supernatural experience without supernatural language is extremely difficult, but I shall try.

7
Ocean of Fire

As I plummet headlong off the top of the trestle . . . I grab for any handle I can grasp . . . scenes blur before my eyes . . . I feel the hopeless sensation of free fall . . . and then I leave my body.

I'm standing by an immense ocean of fire . . . in a darkened sphere of eternity.

The enormous expanse of fire casts an eerie, undulating light against a black sky.

The ocean is like molten lava burning white-hot red, laced with specks of black. Hovering above the turbulence is a six-inch blanket of blue and blue-green flame.

I feel as if the fiery mass is a huge magnet; I am being drawn irrevocably into it, along with a host of other people.

The magnetic force is overwhelming. There is no path back. There is no escape.

Neither I nor anyone else is *in* the vast ocean of fire. I'm standing on its shoreline.

The fear is awesome. On earth I could not comprehend

life or death in an infinity of time.

But my fear here comprehends the antithesis of life after death—death after death. Poof, the sizzling evaporation of a soul. For ever and ever and ever.

My whole being cowers with this new fear within my soul. It is born of the realization, dawning here, a soul can die.

Looking out over that great expanse of fire as far as I can see, I cannot imagine any greater human fear than knowing suddenly you are a victim of this eternal terminal illness.

Prepare a dirge for the saddest holocaust of them all.

As my thoughts reel before the terror of the caldron, I become aware of new values.

Time is different here. It is not measured in increments as on earth. Time just passes. Events happen one after another, but there is no relationship to time.

I get the impression the value of accomplishment is so crucial that it eliminates any value of time. There is no minute, month or century here. It is timeless.

Travel is incredible. You can travel as slowly as you wish. Or with unbelievable speed.

To express it in earth terms, once you've purchased your ticket in your mind, you appear at your destination at the speed of thought, no matter the distance.

One of the other strange things here is that you know everything, not in the encyclopedic sense, but with insight illuminating the knowledge. Your understanding is vast and complete.

You sense a situation and its consequences instantly.

There is no question. This doesn't seem at all startling.

I look again at the burning, turbulent, rolling ocean of fire. Abruptly, very close to me I see two people I know, long since dead on earth.

One is my uncle, Halvor Nomeland, who died of consumption. The other is Ben Grandahl, the boy who was my classmate in school. He died from cancer of the jaw that started with an infected tooth, several years after the death of my uncle. He was only a lad of fifteen.

They look just as they did when they left earth. They seem perplexed and in deep thought as though they cannot believe what they are seeing. Their expressions reflect bewilderment and confusion.

Neither one greets me or speaks to me. But I know we recognize each other. My uncle seems too overcome to speak. Forlornly, he simply shakes his head.

I agree with my uncle, telling him and my friend, "If I'd known it was going to be like this, I would have done anything to keep from coming to this place."

Suddenly I see movement in my peripheral view. As I turn around, a man walks toward us over the turbulent mass of fire. He has a strong, kind, compassionate face.

He is composed. Unafraid. Master of all He sees. He is Jesus Christ.

I know I am in hell. We are lost, confused souls. The three of us are eyewitnesses now to the final judgment.

There is no way back to earth. There is no escape. Except by divine intervention. This is forever.

Looking at Jesus, I know if He will only look at me, a mere glance from Him, and I will go back into that lifeless body in the mill office.

He is my only hope.

I know Jesus didn't have to come to this fury of the final furnace, stoked for holocaust in the maggot-crawling bowels of eternity. He is here because He wants to be here. He knows of my plight. If only He will glance at me.

His eyes are powerful. He looks straight ahead. He walks on by. My heart sinks.

Then He stops. He turns slowly around toward the three of us. His expression does not change. He looks down.

Jesus glances at me. Our eyes meet.

8
The Miracle

Instantly, at the speed of thought, I was back in my body in the mill office.

I heard Mabel praying, but I couldn't move. The press of people were listening to Mabel with eyes riveted on her and me, unaware I was here once again with them.

I felt a stirring of life in my left eyelid.

The gang-sawyer was one of those who had witnessed everything; the fall, search, recovery and what was happening in the mill office. He was a big, tall bull of a man.

He thought this nonsense had gone on long enough; Mabel was just an overemotional, religious woman caught up in shock and grief.

Fifteen minutes had passed since Gunderson pulled my body to the surface of the water. And I had been at the bottom of the pond for at least three quarters of an hour.

It was obvious to all long ago—Tom Welch was dead.

The gang-sawyer thought, "C'm on now, Mabel, you've been given your chance." He understood her Christian faith and her devout desire for me to be raised from the dead. But her prayers simply had not worked.

He was getting ready to usher Mabel out of the office then get on with it and wrap up the body for a trip to a mortuary in Portland, when he was transfixed by the most electrifying jolt of his life.

He sees my eyelids move.

He sees me breathe.

He sees tears fall out of the corners of my eyes.

He sees me open my eyes.

The gang-sawyer recoiled away from me and propelled himself backwards through a door.

In a barely audible voice, I asked, "What happened?"

The people in that mill office knew. They had seen it. At least that which happened at the mill.

They were amazed and stunned. A feeling of consuming, high tension subsided as contagious relief whelmed the atmosphere, and in counterpoint, smiles and tears intermingled as grim exhaustion bottomed out to a growing wave of euphoria.

For they had seen a tragedy. They had seen the violent death of Tom Welch. They had seen a resurrection. They had seen me come back to life.

They had seen a miracle.

As Julius Gunderson related the pervading awe, "I pulled Tom to the surface myself, and witnessed the miracle of life restored in him.

"I thank God for what I saw that day, and I thank God for the privilege of telling it here."

Some assumed I drowned. But no water issued from my mouth.

Gunderson commented, "I was watching for air bubbles or some sign of where he was. I never did see any air bubbles. There was no water in his lungs. He never had breathed in all the time he was underwater."

The ambulance arrived. Attendants put me on a stretcher and loaded me inside. One of them climbed in the rear compartment to take care of me on the thirty-mile ride to Portland.

Fin and Mabel told us they would follow in their car after Fin closed the office, to check me into the hospital officially and remain with me during the crucial first hours.

We started driving down off Larch Mountain. The roads were rough and I was jostled about quite a bit. We passed Half-Way Point, so named because that's where it was, on the four-mile road down the side of the mountain from Palmer Mill to Bridal Veil on the Columbia River.

We finally arrived near Bridal Veil and drove west out of the Columbia Gorge.

Once in Portland the driver turned on his siren. At long last we threaded our way to the emergency entrance at the hospital. This touched off a flurry of activity among nurses, attendants and doctors.

As I was going to learn in a few hours, the final curtain had not descended on the miracle.

Beginning that Monday night until Friday morning I was to be confronted with a question that, depending on my answer, could change the course of the rest of my life.

9

Wheeled Into Surgery

They wheeled me into surgery immediately after the ambulance arrived at Good Samaritan Hospital in Portland.

It was now very late in the afternoon.

Nurses hurriedly cleaned away the blood as doctors began to examine the extent of my injuries.

They determined I had fractured my skull, broken seven ribs on my left side, punctured my left lung, severely lacerated the skin on my head, had no water in my lungs and suffered multiple contusions over my body.

Nurses shaved my head, and a doctor closed with stitches the gaping wounds in my scalp. A turban of bandages was wrapped around my head. Doctors girded my chest with tape, to enable the broken ribs to heal properly over the next six to eight weeks.

Fin and Mabel arrived at the hospital. They supplied the sketchy information necessary to check me in as an official patient and then waited while I was in surgery.

As I was being wheeled out of the operating room on

the way to the intensive care ward, I spotted the Brockes. The nurse stopped long enough for me to talk to them.

Mabel leaned over, "Do you have any pain, Tommy?" I told her, "No."

In fact, as unbelievable as it seemed to me, I suffered no pain at the mill, during the ambulance ride or at the hospital.

I did feel very weak. And very stiff. This caused a kind of paralysis; I could only move my right arm, just a little.

Fin and Mabel walked beside me as the nurse wheeled me to intensive care on the third floor. I asked if I could have something to eat; the nurse brought dinner.

The Brockes stayed for a while longer, then left to return to their home at the mill.

I was now alone. Or, so I thought.

Monday night. Hovering between life and death in the eyes of the doctors. They'd done all they could do. It was simply a matter of wait and see.

But I wasn't alone. The "No Visitors" sign on the door to the intensive care ward had been unceremoniously ignored.

Suddenly, I was acutely aware of the Holy Presence in my room. All this was new to me. Only hours before I had been with Jesus Christ, so now I knew the power of the Holy Spirit. And I felt that power and warmth in my room.

Soon I heard a voice. The voice of the Spirit was unmistakable, very real. He asked me a question He would pose countless times between now and Friday morning, "Will you tell the world what you've seen, and how you came back to life?"

Did I comprehend the meaning of what I'd just heard? I wasn't sure; I'd have to think about it.

My mind was swimming. I'd been through too much to give a hasty answer. Linkages coupled relevant thoughts, weighing the question, my life, what I had seen, what had happened and the meaning of any commitment.

I knew it was presumptuous, but a Socratic answer crossed my mind, "Can I say no, God?"

Tuesday morning Mabel drove from Palmer Mill to Good Samaritan. She said of her visit, "I returned to the hospital the next morning.

"The doctors asked me not to stay long; they did not hold out much hope that he would live."

I smiled to welcome Mabel as she walked toward my bed. In my own mind I was confident I was going to live, but just in case I died again, I was anxious to tell Mabel what had happened to me in the next world.

Talking was difficult. My chest was taped, cinched tight; breathing was shallow. I was wheezing. I was forced to speak slowly with long pauses, but Mabel's burning interest easily stretched her patience to accommodate my halting report.

I sketched the essentials, leaving for later the remainder of my adventure.

I informed Mabel I knew I was dead for a while. I was way off in a wilderness. I was being drawn into something with a lot of other people, as if by a magnet.

I saw my uncle and a boy, a school friend, both of whom had died years ago. There was a big ocean of fire. No one was in the ocean. That was what I was being drawn into; I was afraid, terrified.

Then I saw Jesus coming in the distance. He came closer, passed me and was going on by; I knew, if He would only turn and look at me, He would save me.

His glance would send me from this hopeless place back to the mill office. If not, I felt I was doomed to stay here until the final judgment.

I looked at Mabel and finished at the moment I was raised from the dead, "Then Jesus looked at me and I heard you praying. I opened my eyes as soon as I could and I saw you."

Mabel was astonished. I looked for any facial twitch of skepticism, but there was none. Mabel believed me.

For one thing, she knew me. I had no reason, nor anything to gain, by lying or fabricating a story. She knew that wasn't part of my life anyway.

For another, Mabel was at my side praying for me when the miracle happened on Larch Mountain. Beyond that, she believed what's recorded in the Bible. Her fresh faith left no room for doubt.

Hadn't she been healed of heart disease? Hadn't I been brought back to life before her own eyes?

While I didn't know the significance of what I was telling her, Mabel Brocke knew. I was not aware of the reference or how it was described in the Bible.

Mabel explained that while it looked like an "ocean" to me, Lake Superior would look like an ocean if one just suddenly appeared on its shore. The Scriptures, in the Book of Revelation, say it's a "lake of fire."

The lake contains "fire and brimstone." She had read all about it. I hadn't.

But I had been there. I had seen it.

She quickly related in greater detail what events had taken place at the mill, beginning with my fall from the trestle.

As interesting as our conversation was to Mabel and to me, she remembered the doctors' caution to keep her visit short.

Mabel smiled, laid her right hand on my forehead, paused in silence for a moment, then left. I wouldn't see her again until Friday night.

I settled, in a sense, back in bed; actually, my body remained immobilized.

But my mind was up and about. Clear, alert and active. I had to sift out, weigh, sort, measure, test and examine all that had happened. This can seem overwhelming for a boy of eighteen all alone in the world.

The Holy Spirit continued to communicate with me over the next several days. The question was put to me again and again, "Will you tell the world what you've seen, and how you came back to life?"

The negative aspects of an affirmative answer troubled me seriously.

Would people believe me? Granted, it didn't happen unseen in the middle of an ocean or a desert, or behind closed doors. Of the seventy members of the logging mill's working crew, some had seen me fall, many had witnessed the search and retrieval from the pond, and as many as could had crowded into the mill office and looked on when

I came back to life.

But forty-five minutes underwater, even with eyewitnesses? And not breathing for an hour? Even though I was thoroughly checked for signs of life when I was pulled from the bottom of the mountain pond, and later in the mill office.

Scoffers would challenge, wasn't I really on the surface of the pond, breathing, while the men were searching for me? Wasn't I somehow in an air pocket, breathing underwater, while they were dredging the pond with pike poles? Wasn't there some other plausible, medically acceptable explanation?

And on top of that, Jesus was asking me to tell the world what I'd seen.

Who would believe me? Doubters would explain it away, wasn't that just an ordinary dream, nightmarish perhaps, nonetheless, no more than the stuff of any night's dream?

Hadn't I really read about the lake of fire in the Bible and psychologically years later it surfaced out of my subconscious mind? Didn't I create the ocean of fire in my imagination, albeit the amazing coincidence that it was also in the Bible?

More crucial, wasn't I the only one to journey to the ocean of fire and return? There were no eyewitnesses, except me, to that adventure.

Skeptics would impugn my character.

Was I an opportunist for ends known only to me? Was I a religious fanatic? Was I insane? Was I a liar?

I knew I was none of these; but who else would know?

I knew what I saw and what happened to me; but who would believe me?

10

"Run, Tom, Run!"

Unknown to doctors and nurses, one visitor returned again and again to stay with me unseen in my room at Good Samaritan—the Holy Spirit.

Throughout our many conversations, Jesus and I exchanged questions and replies and comments. He reasoned with me, as a son, to help me unknot my tangles of prejudice, jaundice, hate, paranoia, anger and bitterness until I could thread realities out of what had been a jumbled heap of perceptions in the attic of my mind.

He supplied new bits of colored stone and helped me assemble them until I could see clearly the mosaic of my life.

Jesus would speak, and out of the fog of my ignorance an eternal truth would glimmer and emerge, walking toward me like an old friend to be recognized and welcomed.

"My son, as an eagle may soar free on the wing, a man may soar free on his own will.

"This Holy gift has many chambers which shall now be

opened for your understanding and your wisdom.

"The free will of a man serves him well who scorns it not, for with this sovereign freedom, a man may choose a righteous or evil path, and verily I say unto you: upon the earthly path of your feet God will render a final judgment for the eternal path of your soul.

"Is it not written in Holy Scripture that the small and great shall stand before God; and the books shall be opened, and another book opened which is the book of life; and they shall be judged every man, out of those things written in the books, according to their works; and whosoever is not found written in the book of life shall be cast into the lake of fire?

"Have you not been to the lake of fire and seen it?

"Have I not raised you from the dead?

"Have I not asked you if you will tell the world what you've seen, and how you came back to life?

"My son, you bound your world to that of your father and to that of your mother. In love I say unto you, where stands your world with your father and mother now?

"When a child, you railed against God in a storm of anger at the deaths of your father and mother, gripped near mortally in fear, as a young eagle pushed too soon from the nest.

"Did not your wings give you flight? And for you alone?

"Have I not said that he that loveth father or mother more than me is not worthy of me? and wife, and children, and brethren, and sisters, and yea, his own life also?

"Have I not said, 'He that believeth on me hath everlasting life'?

"Turn not away from my words if they seem harsh; attend to what I say unto you, because it is of my profound love for you and each one on earth, and of my concern for your eternal lives.

"My son, unfettered life in this world and everlasting life in eternity issue from man's free will.

"Be not surprised that worldly shackles abound, sought eagerly by the free, not weighing eternity, but comforting in the moment.

"When man esteems man and the trappings, treasures and pleasures of man, the rewards are for the flesh; the span is temporal; and man's free will is no longer free.

"Has it not been written by an apostle, 'Stand fast therefore in the liberty wherewith Christ hath made us free, and be not entangled again with the yoke of bondage'?

"Have I not said, 'Follow me'?

"Have I not said, 'If ye abide in me, and my words abide in you, ye shall ask what ye will, and it shall be done unto you'?

"Of all worldly relationships, abide in me above all: first, last and always.

"Be not surprised, in this proper order of esteem, other worldly relationships are in fuller measure, in greater love.

"But turn to me, first. Commune with me. Confer with me. You, alone. My guidance and my counsel in all matters, small and great, moment by moment, are for all who walk the earth. I am delighted in those exceedingly whose free will directs them on a righteous path leading to everlasting life.

"Have I not said, 'My sheep hear my voice, and I know them'?

"Have I not said, 'He that is of God heareth God's words'?

"Go not to others and ask them to commune for you with me. It is as foolish to ask others to commune for you, as it is for a man to cleave his world as a barnacle to the world of another man.

"Have I not said, 'Ask, and it shall be given you; seek, and ye shall find; knock, and it shall be opened unto you'?

"Above all, you must believe that I and my Father will provide you everlasting love and guidance in all things, and will never leave you nor forsake you, if you are faithful.

"Do you not believe? Have I not talked with you now, and you heard my voice?"

Indeed. Indeed I have.

I lay there, almost exhausted. It was up to me. I probed my thoughts with increasing intensity. But for some unfathomable reason I couldn't couple the final linkage.

I began to ask what He wanted in my life, "What is your will for me?"

Each time I asked, the response was silence. Absolute silence.

It was now Friday morning. I heard His voice again, "Will you tell the world what you've seen, and how you came back to life?"

At this point only a little time was needed for contemplation. My understanding wended its way out of darkness into victorious light.

I pondered His question to me, and my question of His will for me, which remained unanswered, when all of a sudden, it was so simple!

Of course! His question was His answer!

The supreme moment arrived in my life.

At eleven-thirty I made my decision, my commitment. I harbored not a shred of reservation.

I asked the nurse to leave my room for a while. She was reluctant, but I explained I wanted to be alone for a few moments, "I'll be all right."

The nurse hesitated out of concern; she knew I was virtually helpless. But she agreed, adjusted a screen in front of the door, and rustled out.

I surveyed my condition. How could I possibly get up?

I had a severely injured head. I had no idea whether any brain damage had resulted from the skull fracture, or whether I'd be risking permanent impairment if I tried to walk. I had broken ribs and a punctured lung, and I knew that any movement might exacerbate those injuries.

I was still so weak and stiff I could only move my right arm. I didn't know the extent of my progress in recovery, other than the obvious fact I was still in the intensive care ward.

In a gesture of hand-raising despair at my own inability to respond, I spoke out to the presence of God in my room, "Lord, if that is what You want me to do, I'll do my best. I'll tell the world what I've seen, and how I came back to life.

"But I can't do it lying here. You'll have to get me out of this place."

Immediately I felt the sensation of a glow tingle the top of my head.

As light precedes a candle and grows with brightness at the approach of the flame, so, too, a Holy warmth wafted down through every fiber and cell of my body.

Torn flesh is knit. Fissured bones are fused.

The touch is unmistakable. I'm healed.

Mabel had left a battered old suitcase containing some of my clothes under the bed when she visited Tuesday. I jumped into my clothing as quickly as possible, buttoning the pair of jeans over my shirt.

I pulled on my boots, and with a hasty buckle of my belt, I grabbed the suitcase and headed for the door.

I peeked around the door, with my turban of bandages extending farther than I would have wished, checking the corridor in both directions. It was empty. The coast was clear.

"Run, Tom, run!" shoots a thought-meteor across my mind.

I looked across the way at two signs. One said "Elevator" and the other said "Stairs." Where I grew up in Canada, we didn't know anything about elevators, so I took the stairs. I hurried down several flights of steps, through a door, and out onto Marshall Street.

All this time I was afraid the nurse or the staff would spot me, throw a net over me or whatever they do and force me back into the hospital.

One can't just get up and leave an intensive care ward without official release.

How could I explain the healing?

I couldn't. They'd think I wasn't playing with a full deck. They'd think I was out of my mind.

More thought-meteors on the run. I'd better go someplace fast. I was too easy a target to detect with my head all bandaged up and lugging this battered old suitcase.

I thought of a friend of mine, Pete Burness. He had a printing shop near Good Sam.

I rushed to his shop and ran inside to safety.

Now, Pete was unflappable. He served with the Canadian Army under the British during World War I and had been decorated with some distinguished medals for bravery, including the Victoria Cross.

He turned around, looked at me and remarked in his typically understated way. "Well, I see you're out."

I responded, "Yes," and then sketched my predicament. He was helpful instantly. Pete tossed his car keys to me, "Go down to the house. I'll ride the streetcar home today."

He paused, looked at the grotesque sight in front of him and offered a few words of advice, "When you get home, you'd better stick there, as long as you're bandaged up in such a bloody mess."

I drove to Pete's home. As I parked his car in the driveway, Mabel Burness, Pete's daughter, glanced out of the kitchen door and saw me.

Mabel was ten years of age. She had been in the vicinity

of the logging mill trestle on Monday when I fell, and she had watched the men search for me in the pond. After I was retrieved, young Mabel had gone with Fin to get her Aunt May to pray for me in the mill office.

Also now staring out of the kitchen door was Pete's wife, Charlotte "Lottie" Burness, the sister of Mabel Brocke.

According to Mabel Burness, "Mother and I were talking in the kitchen. I looked out of the door and said, 'Mother, there's Tom.'

"She said, 'No it isn't. It can't be. He's in the hospital.'

"He came in and sat down on the end of the kitchen table, which was next to the door. Mother threw up her hands and said, 'Tom! What are you doing here?' Tom answered, 'I've been healed.'

"It was quite a surprise to see him, because we had just been talking about going to the hospital to visit him. With his head all wrapped up in a turban we expected somebody from Good Samaritan to come and get him.

"I told him, 'If anyone is healed I've got to see that it's true.' He said, 'It is. I'll show you.'

"He sat down and started taking off his bandages. After he got them off, there were all these black stitches sticking up in his scalp. I told him, 'You've got stitches in your head.'

"He went in the other room, took out the stitches, washed his head as if nothing had happened and came back to show us. He told us about the other injuries and the complete healing in the hospital.

"He *was* healed. It was a miracle."

After Mabel's comment about the stitches in my head, I wanted to see for myself, so I went to Pete's room to look in the dresser mirror. What a ghastly sight!

I was a mess. My hair had been shaved off on top. Stitches were everywhere.

I started the job of putting me back together again. I grabbed Pete's comb and forced it through the unkempt hair that had been left on the sides. Unfortunately the comb caught a stitch. Blood oozed out around the suture.

As I looked at the bleeding in the mirror, I heard a voice say, "You are *not* healed."

I stopped, transfixed, for several moments looking at myself. Then I noticed Pete's safety razor. I took the blade and, with tweezers, cut and removed every stitch. There was no more bleeding. I was sure now. I was healed.

But that voice. That chilling, maniacal voice. I had never heard it before.

Although I had no way of knowing then, I was going to hear it again in the next few weeks. It would threaten my life.

I took off the tape from around my chest. After some time of cleaning up, I drove downtown to see Dr. Brewer, the physician assigned to me at Good Samaritan.

11

"How Did You Get Out of the Hospital?"

For any casual observer, I'm afraid the oddity of my appearance disguised the solemnity of my mission.

I dashed in off the street into Dr. Brewer's office, the fugitive patient, a bizarrely barbered, bald headed young man.

Startled, Dr. Brewer stood up. "What in the world are you doing here?" He didn't give me a chance to answer.

"Are you all right? How did you get out of the hospital?"

"Dr. Brewer, I ran out. I didn't tell anyone at Good Samaritan I was leaving. They're probably still looking for me."

"I'm sure they are. Tell me what happened."

I took a deep breath. "Doctor, the Lord has healed me and I'm all right now."

He came closer, pressed in on my ribs that had been broken and frowned, "Didn't that hurt?"

I told him, "No." It was true; there was no pain.

He looked up at my head, "Who removed the stitches from your scalp?" I responded that I had removed them, and how I had done it.

Then I told him my concern, why I was there.

"This morning I made a commitment to God, to tell people how I died at the mill, where I went when I was dead, about the ocean of fire and how I came back to life.

"A few hours ago God healed me so I could get out of that hospital bed.

"There will be some, perhaps many, who will doubt what I tell them. Fin and Mabel Brocke and others were at the mill. They know what happened and they will tell, I'm sure, how it all took place.

"There will be those who will probably ask for the name of my doctor, and I will, of course, give them your name.

"Dr. Brewer, it's important to me to know what you're going to tell them about my death and my healing this morning."

There was silence. Dr. Brewer seemed to be weighing caution as he was putting together a proper response to me.

Slowly he began, "Well, I can only speak from what I know as your doctor. Mrs. Brocke and you have told me about what happened up there at the mill.

"She said you were underwater for forty-five minutes, maybe an hour, after you fell and hit some supports of a logging structure.

"From our examination, with an absence of water in your lungs, I can only conclude from what I've been told about the length of time you were supposed to have been underwater, and I know nothing about that, but let's say that was the case, then, with no water in your lungs, you died when your head hit the bridgework during your fall.

"You did not breathe underwater. You would have been dead when you went into the water.

"I must tell you I'm not aware of anyone living after being underwater for that period of time." The repeated, exaggerated facial expressions unmasked the physician's scientific skepticism.

"Now, about what you say happened this morning in the hospital. If you say you had a healing, somewhat instantly as you've indicated, of God, then God must have healed you this morning, because I know we didn't.

"Usually it takes anywhere from six to eight weeks for broken ribs to heal, when everything goes well. Today you have been in the hospital, let's see, four days.

"Of course I haven't given you an examination, but you don't seem to have any discernible effects from the skull fracture or the lung puncture.

"I guess I'd have to say your recovery has been rather remarkable."

I had heard what I wanted to know. I thanked Dr. Brewer and drove back to Pete's home.

In the evening the Brockes came to Portland looking for me. They had visited Good Samaritan, only to learn I was gone. Mabel phoned Lottie to ask if she knew my whereabouts, and Lottie told her I was with them.

They rushed over to find out what had happened to me. They were delighted to hear about the healing. They asked me if I wanted to return home with them to the mill that night.

I told them, "Yes."

12
Zero Hour, Tell the World

Saturday morning dawned bright, clear and beautiful over Larch Mountain. After breakfast Fin and I walked over to the mill.

I was returning to work.

Tom Welch? Back at work? The men of the crew reeled from the news. They couldn't believe their eyes when they saw me.

Other than my bald head, I didn't look much different than when I reported for work Monday morning. But the crew remembered the last Tom Welch they saw, the battered, crumpled corpse they pulled from the bottom of the pond.

Only I knew I *was* different, and why. Between the bookends of Monday and Friday, the wisdom of wisdom had been given to me in one short, cataclysmic sweep.

Wherever I went, clusters of men stopped me. "Hey, Tom, how can you be back on the job? You're supposed to be in the hospital. What are you doing here?"

"It's good to see you, Tom. We saw what happened,

when you were in the office, too. Why don't you tell us about it?"

"Mabel said you were at a lake of fire. Is that true?"

"What happened in the hospital? Someone said this morning you were healed; it was another miracle after the miracle when you came back to life."

"I can't believe you're here, Tom. Do you remember being in the pond, anything about it?"

The questions tumbled out as groups gathered around me.

It should have come as no surprise to me, but it did. I was the number-one topic of news and conversation during the week. People were genuinely interested.

They went to Mabel, and she told them of her conversations with the doctors and with me. Word spread faster than German measles, not only among the crew but to their families. Everyone was trying to put together bits and pieces of information.

And now, as I went about my duties, they wanted to hear all the details from me. It was obvious I couldn't tell everything to each one individually, and, with an eye to Fin, we were not getting any work done, either. So I told them, "If you'll gather in the schoolhouse tomorrow night, Sunday night, I'll tell you what happened, the whole story."

This would be a small step, I thought to myself, but it would be a beginning. I was going forth to tell the world.

On the seventh day, Sunday night, just before eight o'clock, I approached the little schoolhouse.

I was surprised to see a large crowd. Something else

must be going on. As it sank in that this large crowd was here for me, I panicked.

I almost turned and ran. But I couldn't back out now. I entered the room and edged my way up to the front.

Good Lord, the room was full of people. Not only that, others were peering in the doors and windows. I guess the room could accommodate about eighty, but the whole crowd looked to be about one hundred and twenty-five. The entire mill crew must have been there with their families and guests. Outside, it was getting dark.

At eight o'clock Fin Brocke got up, said a few words of welcome, sang a hymn, led us in prayer and introduced me.

My zero hour had arrived.

The preliminaries seemed to go entirely too fast for me. There was an awkward delay. Fin sat down. I didn't want to stand up. I was nervous. I wasn't at all sure what I should do.

I had been comfortable as a loner in the Alberta wilderness. Never had I been packed into a room with so many people looking at me.

And I was supposed to *talk*. As I stood up behind the teacher's desk, all of a sudden a supernatural peace and calm engulfed me, washing away the fear and panic.

The same beautiful Presence which had been with me in Good Samaritan's intensive care ward was with me now, filling the air in and around the little schoolhouse.

I opened my mouth to speak. Thoughts and words flooded my mind. They were not of me. They were of the Holy Spirit. I spoke them as they came.

I told the men of the mill where I had been when they

were dredging and retrieving my body from the pond and while my corpse lay in the mill office.

I explained how I had been sent from death to life by the power of a mere glance from Jesus Christ. I described the ocean of fire.

I related everything that had happened in the hospital. About hearing the voice of God, "Will you tell the world what you've seen, and how you came back to life?" About my solemn commitment, and the instant healing.

I now knew firsthand, so I told them, of God's love for each and every one of us. I warned them of the judgment to come, how to prepare for it, how to escape the lake of fire and how their lives might become eternal.

After the meeting, as we were walking home, I asked Fin and Mabel about some of the words and phrases I had spoken. I had no idea what I was saying was in the Bible.

Later that night Fin got the Holy Scriptures and showed me. Lo and behold, there were the very words.

My audience in the schoolhouse listened intently. The meeting lasted no more than thirty minutes. But at the end, when I finished, there was a reverent silence unequaled in my experience.

When I fell to my death, these men were there. They knew what happened; they had seen the resurrection. They had seen the miracle.

I had begun to fulfill my commitment to God. I didn't know until later what effect it would have on their lives.

Mabel knew, because she had been told, "For the glory of God."

But there was one who was cynical. We didn't know what was about to happen to him.

13
One Mocked

Only an unthinking person could whistle past the graveyard at the personal implications of the miracle.

It was a time in the lives of all those at Palmer Mill to reckon with God. Some went forward to seek God immediately, some continued in serious introspection, and one mocked the miracle.

Surprisingly, it was Jimmy Gaydon. He and Fin had worked out all the engineering refinements on the production chain at the mill. They were good friends. He had been exposed to Fin's very strong faith. And based on that, I suppose I had taken Jimmy's faith for granted; that's the only way I can explain why I was so shocked at his reaction.

Not only was Jimmy at work the day I fell, he was operating the huge carriage saw not far from me on the top deck of the trestle. He saw me fall, and he was one of those who had taken part in the search for my body.

Jimmy got acquainted with me well enough to know I was ignorant of the Bible and religious life.

He had attended the meeting in the schoolhouse on Sunday night. His information was accurate and complete, not distorted by grapevine accounts, which made his irrational scorn incredible to me.

For reasons of his own, after what must have been earnest soul searching, Jimmy noised some strong, mocking remarks among the crew, "After something happens, those religious folks step up and say a prayer did this or a prayer did that, and they say they knew it would all the time, and I mean *after* something happens.

"They say the Lord raised Tom up. Oh, it's a miracle, they say. They haven't got any proof. How do we know that? I don't believe it. Satan's got power, too. The Bible says he does. I'd sooner believe it was the work of Satan. You can believe what you want; I believe it was the work of Satan."

On the tenth day, the Wednesday following the meeting at the schoolhouse, Jimmy and his wife rose early as usual.

Jimmy must have had a strong premonition, because during breakfast he informed his wife, "When you hear the emergency whistle blow today, I'll be dead." She dismissed the comment as being overly dramatic, perhaps born out of a mood of depression.

Jimmy reported for work at the main saw on the top of the trestle. Later in the morning he slabbed a log about forty feet long.

After squaring it up, he cut it down the middle. He finished off one half and backed it off, he thought, onto the original loader, so he could finish off the other half.

The half he thought he backed off caught on the tail block of the carriage. When he brought the carriage forward with a surge of great power, the first half was propelled off the carriage, toward Jimmy's safety cage.

The gang-sawyer saw the crisis and rushed over to try to stop the carriage, when the huge timber caromed off, sailed through the air, crushed the safety cage, broke Jimmy's neck and killed him.

For the second time in two weeks a distress call was rushed to the office and the emergency whistle shut down the mill and shrieked catastrophe for all hands and families to hear, including Jimmy's wife, at eleven o'clock.

She rushed out of the house, joining several people on their way to the mill, and said with certainty, "Jimmy's dead. He told me this was going to happen before he left for work."

Jimmy's tragedy had a frightening impact on the men at the mill and their families. After they digested what had happened to me and to Jimmy, within three months most of those who were teetering went forward to God for salvation.

God is not mocked.

When I was at the home of Pete Burness taking out my stitches, blood had oozed out from the first stitch I caught in the comb, and a chilling voice had taunted me, "You are *not* healed."

That voice was going to threaten me unexpectedly in a few days, the following Monday night.

14

"I'm Going to Kill You"

Today marked the third week of my reporting for work at Palmer Mill. How could so much happen in so short a period of time?

I wondered what was going to happen this week. My wait would not be long.

With church services yesterday, the last place most people would expect the Brockes to go today would be to a prayer meeting, but on this Monday evening that was exactly where they were going. They invited me to attend, along with some friends.

The meeting would be held in the home of Charlie Nordling, the flume tender, at Half-Way Point, between the mill and Bridal Veil, where there was a small community of homes.

I begged off. "Fin, I really don't feel like going. I'll just stay home and watch after Marjorie and Happy and George. Don't worry about us, we'll be okay."

After playing awhile, the Brocke children wound down, tired and drowsy, earlier than usual. Sometime after eight o'clock I tucked them into bed.

I strolled down to my bedroom, turned on the light, sat down on my bed and casually took off one boot, when my hairs started to rise. I couldn't believe what I was seeing.

Suddenly, right through the side of the house, right through the bedroom wall, appeared this monster of a man. He was as tall as the ceiling, nine feet. He was a brawny, athletic, handsome human being; he was in a crouched position.

Having acquired an outdoor survival instinct in the Canadian wilds, the moment I sense danger, like animals, I freeze. That's exactly what I did; only my eyes moved, riveted to him.

The giant raised his arms up to his shoulders and stretched out his hands toward me in a choking fashion.

Then I heard the same, low, chilling voice I heard when I was removing my stitches in front of Pete's mirror.

The voice said, "I'm going to kill you. I'm the devil."

I wasn't asleep; I wasn't dreaming; I wasn't insane. My hairs still stood on end.

Thoughts crowded out one another for attention, "You've got to do what you heard at the prayer meetings. This is really happening. You're cornered; you've got to do something. I know it's not a human person, I know that, even though I'm looking right at a human person."

So I said it, blurted it out, "I rebuke you, devil, in the name of Jesus."

I really didn't know what to expect, but nothing happened. He didn't move.

Then a strange thing occurred. Something gave me

supernatural vision to see inside this huge, malignant creature. I literally looked right inside him, as a living X-ray, in the area of his stomach.

His organs were trembling and shaking.

I examined him closely. I told him, "You're the fellow who's afraid. What I'm saying apparently is having some effect on you."

He didn't move, either to come farther into the room or to leave. He just stood there, crouched.

He could have pinched my head off between his thumb and forefinger. I knew that.

But with my rebuke, he wasn't going to kill me like he said he would; he couldn't kill me.

I stood up. A midget by comparison. I pointed my finger and commanded, "Devil, that's where you came in. In the name of Jesus, that's where you'd better go out. Leave this room, now."

Satan backed out and vanished.

My encounter was over in a matter of minutes, but I stood there for some time, one boot on and one boot off.

Then I sat down on the bed thinking, "Boy! Nobody on earth will ever believe anything like this. I won't tell anybody. That's the best way. Just forget it."

For some odd reason the Brockes didn't stay at the prayer meeting as long as they indicated they would. I heard Fin's Chevrolet pull up and park; they had been gone about an hour and a half. I took off the other boot, turned out the light and lay down.

They approached the house. Fin stepped inside the door, paused and then called back to Mabel, who was still outside with their guests, "Mama, there's something wrong here. It feels to me like the devil has been in this house."

Fin entered my room, turned on the light and looked down at me. I was playing possum. I'd made up my mind; I was not going to tell any of this stuff. No one was going to accuse me of being insane, or of being a fool.

But Fin had a supernatural discernment. And I couldn't lie to him.

"Tom, I know you're not asleep." I said, "No." He didn't take his eyes off me, "What's happened here?" I told him, "I heard what you said when you came in the door."

"Is it true? Tell me what happened." I told him everything.

He could see I was disturbed. I paused, "I know that sounds like . . ." and Fin interrupted, "Now, just a minute. In the first place, we believe you.

"We had a short prayer meeting because something hurried us home again." His friend added, "You see, we sensed something like this during prayer and coming up the road."

That week Fin and Mabel convened the prayer group after Fin declared, "We're going to get together and in the name of God rebuke this thing so it won't affect people here again."

They did. And that was the last time Satan appeared while I was there. When the weakest saint is on his knees, he doesn't know how strong he is.

Four young interns of the clergy would soon be on their knees, too, not one of us knowing the epoch events God was about to reveal to us.

15
Prophetic Words at El Cajon

Unknown to me, a minister sat in the audience at the schoolhouse near Palmer Mill on the Sunday evening I first told my story.

Reverend Pitts invited me to talk to the congregation of his church, in the Portland suburb of Gresham, one Sunday afternoon.

The Brockes accompanied me. They agreed with me that an audience could easily scoff at the unbelievable series of events and my incredible experiences unless eyewitnesses were there to corroborate them.

And who better than the Brockes? They had been with me all the way.

The church was packed, and the meeting went as well as the one in the schoolhouse.

Again, the clergy was present. Sprinkled throughout the crowd were five ministers who had heard about the miracle on Larch Mountain.

I was invited to some of their churches, and as I related the miracle to each additional audience, the Brockes readily substantiated what I said, adding the interesting aspects of their own accounts of their roles in the story.

And so it went. I was now launched into my commitment to God to tell the world what I had seen and how I came back to life. The launching was not that of an ocean liner, I can assure you; it was more that of a rowboat, and the oars were mine.

I quit my job at the mill. In doing so, I made the first big, important decision in my life about money. A number of well-intentioned people felt sorry for me and advised me to file a lawsuit against the company, "Those working conditions are terrible; they're not safe. There should be a guardrail up there on that trestle. I'll bet the company won't let Fin spend the money.

"You'd get a lot of money out of a lawsuit even if they just settle with you, Tom."

I went back to commune with Jesus about that one, and I was promptly told I was whole; my understanding and wisdom had increased and matured beyond measure; how could I justify permanent injury when I had been brought back to life and healed instantly in Good Samaritan hospital?

The company and I agreed on twenty-seven dollars. Four and a half days' wages, for Monday until noon Friday. I wouldn't agree to any wages for Friday afternoon; I was well, able to work, but not working. They would pay the bills of the doctor and the hospital.

The Lord was right. I was alive, healed, in top physical condition.

I had been chosen for a miracle at the tender age of

eighteen. How many in all the world have been chosen to go to the lake of fire and chosen for a resurrection by a mere glance from Jesus?

My decision was sound. It would guide me for the rest of my life. God had a purpose for this miracle, and it was not to be tainted with gain from trumped-up lawsuits or any medicine-show commercialism. Of one thing I was quite certain; there was to be no profiteering on this miracle. I was simply to be the witness and the evangelist.

In telling my story to audience after audience I became painfully aware I was not well-grounded in theology. Therefore I involved myself full-time in Dr. Lake's church in Portland, studying under his wing for the ministry.

A group of four enthusiastic young bucks assembled at this time in Portland, all anxious to start our ministries: Gordon Lindsay, Leon Hall, Lawrence Myreen and me.

We began holding meetings on the street at Fourth and Washington. Sometimes the services were a prelude to the evening prayer meetings in the church.

One evening we were on the corner. Leon was preaching, and a crowd gathered. Pretty soon a Chinese gentleman walked up, stopped and observed.

I recognized him. He ran a lottery gambling operation out of a clandestine office not far away on Third Avenue. One had to obtain a coded pass to get into the gaming room; I knew because I was given one and went in just to look around, I suppose out of a desire to confront sin where it lives.

This man was prominent not only in Portland's

Chinatown; his reputation as a well-known gambler around the community was well established, too.

He stood there on the sidewalk and listened for a while. He was carrying a cane with a gold head on it, to be used for more than one purpose, if necessary.

After the sidewalk sermon he seemed in no hurry to leave, so I walked over and talked with him.

"That was a good message," he said. "I know you know who I am, and maybe a little surprised I'm interested in what you people have to say." I responded, "Well, we're having a service inside the church. It's already begun, but we'd like to have you join us." He nodded; the Chinese gambler and I walked inside.

It was Sunday night. After a while Myreen, who had a fabulous gift of tongues and interpretation, stood up and began speaking in a tongue unknown to me.

My companion leaned over, "Where did this man learn to speak Chinese?"

I whispered back, "I don't think he's studied, or knows, the language. We'll find out. Let's ask him."

"He's talking in a very high dialect from my part of China," the man continued. "Sir," I responded, "God must want you to hear this message, because I'm sure my friend doesn't know anything about Chinese."

Myreen finished, joined us and confirmed my supposition, "I don't know how to speak Chinese. This is the Holy Spirit talking through me." There was no need for English interpretation.

The translator understood every word, "You were telling me I should surrender my life to God and return to my people in my province in China, to help them solve some difficult problems they are now facing."

He stood there pensive, humble. A dewy look formed in his eyes as he turned to us, "This must be coming from God direct to me with great meaning, and I'd better do something about it."

He walked forward, knelt down at the altar and gave himself to God. Four months later, after attending church regularly, he returned to China. We never heard from him again.

During this time Reverend Lake ordained me a minister, having completed my study in his nondenominational church in Portland.

It was now February, 1926, not quite two years after the miracle, when Dr. Lake and the church dispatched Lindsay, Hall and me down to southern California, as affiliates of their mission in San Diego.

We worked there for a while before we set up a tent in El Cajon, an area we determined in our youthful exuberance to be a spiritually dry desert. El Cajon is just east of San Diego. We started our first tent revival meetings in the spring.

Some exciting things happened in El Cajon. There was a man in town who owned the lumber yard and was distinguished by his awkward gait. He had a club foot. It was an awful-looking thing.

He attended our services regularly. One night he came forward and asked us to pray for a healing. The three of us laid hands on him and prayed for a healing, but nothing happened.

Leon prayed for a healing at each service. Gordon and I continued to pray for the man, too, but in all candor, we had given up. We thought Leon was going to embarrass us all if he persisted.

I felt like telling Leon, "If you keep that up, no one's going to believe us. Why don't you just let it go?" But I didn't say anything.

We hid in the wings whenever Leon prayed for him. I would have ducked behind one of the tent poles if it would have covered me.

Leon persisted, and one night, suddenly, the man's ankle just loosened out. It was normal. Like the other one. He was healed.

Needless to say, Gordon and I came out from behind our curtained faith.

Bob Keaton had been a middleweight boxer in the state of Colorado. He brought his wife and two daughters to our services.

About this time some kids had been giving us problems in the back of the tent. One of them, a young man, would pull his pants above his knees, stand on his head on the seat and stick his feet up in the air.

One night I told Gordon, "If that kid does that again, I'm going to go back there and do what I have to do."

During the service I looked their way and sure enough, there was this kid on his head with his feet sticking up in the air. The tent was forty by sixty feet and was crowded with two hundred people.

The kid didn't notice me as I hurried down the center aisle. I didn't know what I was going to do, yet. When I

Courtesy of Oregon Historical Society

Palmer Mill, circa 1924

Palmer logging pond on Larch Mountain. The train is loaded
with logs, and can be seen on the trestle in middle of picture. The chute, which runs diagonally across the picture
into the pond, was used for sending logs into the pond from
a "donkey" loading dock farther up the mountain.

Palmer Mill, circa 1924

Steam engine locomotive with train engineer standing in
the door of cab. Palmer logging pond on Larch Mountain
in the background. Trains were used by the Bridal Veil
Lumber Company to move logs to holding pond.

Thomas Welch fell to his violent death from the top of a
trestle nearby.

<u>Left to right</u>: Leon Hall, Thomas Welch, Gordon Lindsay

Picture taken in January 1926, in Portland, Oregon, just before the young evangelistic team (each about 20 years of age) left for their firebrand revival crusade of faith, salvation, and healing held over a period of 4 months in a tent in El Cajon, near San Diego, California.

"Those are three of the rawest evangelistic recruits for God you'll ever see" Thomas Welch

Picture of tent used for evangelistic crusade in Portand, Oregon by Reverend Welch in 1946. This tent would seat 1,000 people.

<u>Left to right</u>: Gordon Lindsay, Leon Hall, Thomas Welch

This is the last picture taken of the three evangelists together. It was taken in 1972. Gordon Lindsay died in 1973, and Leon Hall in 1979.

Gretta Welch and Reverend Thomas Welch.

Picture taken in 1977.

Laura Lee's endorsement appears on the first page of this book. As a truly remarkable woman, alive through miracles in her life, *The Oregonian* headline read, "Laura Lee sees peace after 'walk through fire' ". She has lived an "emotion packed" life of "great extremes".

Laura Lee, authoress of 4 books, had appeared on television interview shows, and had been the "belle of the literary world." She had traveled internationally as well as throughout the United States. Stricken with Hodgkin's disease, she valiantly held off chemotherapy until her third child was born. Now she is triumphant after her therapy and is presently touring the Ukraine.

Mrs. Freda Lindsay, wife of Reverend Gordon Lindsay, and co-founder of "Christ for the Nations, International", based in Dallas, Texas.

> "My late husband, Reverend Gordon Lindsay, called the story of Thomas Welch 'one of the greatest miracles of the twentieth century'"
> The miracle lives on in their ministry.

Mrs. Lindsay's world-wide missions ministry has helped construct 10,000 churches and 31 schools around the world. Over 26,000 students have graduated from their campus and are now active in their own international mission work.

got there, I yanked the seat out from under him, and he fell off into the sawdust. I was hoping he'd get up fighting mad. Which he did. But I noticed he wasn't looking at me. He was looking past me at someone else.

I didn't move. Then I felt this hand on my shoulder. It was Bob Keaton. "Preacher," he said, "I'm going to do your fighting."

Then he asked the ringleader of the troublemakers, "Do you know who I am?" to which the fellow said, "Yeah, I know who you are." Bob spaced out his words forcefully, "Don't ever let me see your face in here again." They left.

Bob turned around, "I guess I'm going to have to get into this and protect you fellows." Later in the evening he gave himself to God. Soon after, his wife and daughters did, too.

In another service Bob came forward for us to pray for a healing for him. A doctor had determined there was a tumor in his stomach. We prayed for his healing and suggested he go back to his doctor for another examination. The doctor confirmed within the constraints of medical science that Bob Keaton was healed in our tent service by the Lord in El Cajon.

Not long after this, one afternoon Gordon and I were deep into a major job of rebuilding our Chevrolet engine; we were crouched over the front fenders with our heads and hands stuck deep in the engine area, like surgeons operating on a very sick friend.

We heard the approaching shuffle of our crotchety old neighbor, whose favorite pastime was to argue with us about religion, doctrine and the Bible.

He delighted in baiting us on stories in the Scriptures, convinced without question they could not possibly be open to literal interpretation; they could only be allegorical.

We were hospitable. A conversation ensued. For no particular reason, the story of Jonah entered the discussion.

"You don't believe such a ridiculous yarn? You look like intelligent boys to me."

We admitted, "Yes, we believe the story exactly as it's told in the Bible."

He drew back, "Well, then, how could Jonah be swallowed by a whale, survive, live three days in the whale's belly and come out alive?"

Gordon responded, "I don't know exactly how it all happened.

"But I know that God can perform any miracle that's necessary to accomplish His purpose.

"When I get to heaven I'll ask Jonah to explain the mysteries about it."

To which the old man tweaked Gordon's nose, "But, suppose Jonah didn't go to heaven?"

To which Gordon pointed downward and responded, "Then you can ask him."

The grouch harrumphed and shuffled away; we smiled at each other and went back to work on the engine.

In July we heard that a firebrand Christian, whose ministry included prophecy and interpretation, had run afoul of religious ideological differences in Mexico. He was under house arrest just across the border from San Diego in Tijuana.

Gordon Lindsay and I decided to see what we could do to extricate him from his predicament. We concluded the only thing to do was cross the international border on a daring raid to rescue "Pete" Peterson.

Gordon and I drove our "four-ninety" Chevrolet into Tijuana, found Pete and received a briefing on the situation from a Mexican taxi driver in whose house the government had assigned him for detention.

Pete had never heard of us, but he welcomed our mission, which we soon learned was not just a simple matter of getting *him* out. He had boxes of equipment in the form of slides and projectors. How could we get this stuff across the border without having everything confiscated or, worse, being detained or arrested ourselves?

After explaining the situation, Pete's host outlined a tactical plan, "You load Pete's luggage and equipment in your car.

"He'll ride with me. I'll leave first. You delay and follow later. I can get him across the border, because the Mexican and American guards know me.

"I'll drive for a while toward San Diego and pull off on the right side of the road, where Pete can transfer to your car after you get across.

"Don't worry about any further action. My government won't press any charges. This is not a matter of interest to the police. This is a matter of honest difference about religious doctrine."

Gordon and I approached the checkpoint with all of Pete's luggage and equipment in the back seat, covered just enough with a blanket to show some of the boxes and suitcases, so no one would get the idea we were trying to hide anything.

We drove up behind a Cadillac limousine as the emigration officer walked to the car. A well-dressed man and woman were in the back seat, separated by a window and quite a length of car from the chauffeur.

It was a steaming July day. Heat waves rose cobra fashion out of the pavement.

The official at the Mexican line asked the couple to get out of the car. These were days of "prohibition." United States law prohibited the possession of liquor, and Mexico searched suspicious automobiles to prevent smuggling.

The couple couldn't get out of the car under their own power; they were too drunk. We discovered later the man was an American banker in San Diego.

The guard shouted at him loud enough for us to hear, "You get out or I'm going to pull you out." And pull him out he did.

The man couldn't stand up. He sprawled on the pavement.

The officer walked around to the woman's door and repeated what he said to her companion. She was as drunk as he. The officer pulled her out.

The woman couldn't stand up. She sprawled on the pavement.

What a sight. There they both lay in the road right in front of our car.

Gordon and I looked at each other, not at all irritated by the delay. We sensed this diversion might be very helpful to our clearance at the checkpoint.

The chauffeur was told to help the man and woman back into the car, which he did, and then to pull the car out of line to the right for further investigation.

I looked out of the driver's window behind us to see a long line of traffic stopped bumper to bumper up the grade all the way back into Tijuana.

Pete and the taxi driver had already crossed the border.

I put the Chevrolet in first gear. It was now our turn. The Mexican official glanced at his watch. Then he stared at the long line of waiting cars. He was fuming. Gordon was praying.

The confusion, delay and heat weighed heavily on the officer. He erupted and barked at me, "What are you doing over here?"

I whistled meekly, "Oh, we're just over here looking around." He surveyed the back seat, all the while talking in Spanish, which I'm sure included some choice epithets about American tourists.

He turned back to me. "I want to see the tail of this car down that road. Look what you're holding up back there. Get out of here." His hand blurred in motion as he waved us on. He didn't have to ask me a second time.

We spotted the Tijuana taxi down the road, and we thanked its owner for all his help as Pete transferred to our car.

Back in our tent in El Cajon during the evening, our services were particularly inspirational; we were delighted to have Pete with us.

Sometime after midnight we returned to our quarters,

a small home. For some reason none of us was exhausted or even talking of going to bed; we were still riding the crest of the exhilaration of the revival service.

After a while Lindsay, Hall, Peterson and I began to pray. We knelt in the front room of our home; it was now about three o'clock.

Soon Pete began to speak in a foreign tongue. As he did, a warm glow filled the room and the house. Unquestionably, we four knew we were in the presence of God, encapsulated and at once exalted by the Holy Spirit.

Leon interpreted sections of a prophecy as it was revealed to Pete.

God told us there was going to be a time of great famine, poverty, suffering, hunger and starvation.

God told us there was going to be a war in which great nations of the world would collide—with unbelievable destruction, bloodshed and death—over a period of many years.

God told us there would be a falling away—like Simon the sorcerer—of the gifts of the Spirit (healing, knowledge, wisdom, faith, miracles, prophecy, discernment, tongues and interpretation of tongues). Mankind would succumb to the love of money and power—the reckless gratification of esteem, self, sexual appetites—and all the pleasures of the senses. Unbelief would sweep the earth. Men who have had the gifts of God in their lives at an earlier time would no longer believe. We were told many times, "They that believe will believe no more."

God told us, after a drought in the gifts of the Spirit, there would be a restoration—a great outpouring of the gifts of the Spirit—through churches and especially through individuals and lay people, all over the world. And we were told, "If you're faithful. . . if you're faithful . . . if you're faithful . . . you will live to see this great renewal in the gifts of the Spirit and have a part in it."

God told us there would be another great war, visiting upon the earth the most violent holocaust the world had ever seen. The world would be divided into two warring camps, those of God in one and the godless in the other. Death, disease, hunger, starvation, sickness, confusion, destruction and suffering would cover the earth on a scale never before seen. One-third of the population of the world would perish. God then told us that from the ashes, the North American civilization would rise to unassailable power, and on that continent there would be a rebirth of spiritual and intellectual holiness which would lead the world to greater wisdom, understanding, knowledge and love in God. Therein would be the power—in God's love—in the Holy Spirit. God told us that in this time He would pour out and spread His Spirit throughout His people.

The four of us were stunned. We couldn't comprehend what all this meant; this was pretty heady stuff.

At about twenty years of age we were too young to have experienced anything remotely similar to these prophetic events. Nonetheless, even men of God so young could not mistake the cosmic magnitude of being witness to things to come.

I had been again in the Holy Presence. I knew the omniscience. I knew the power. I knew the love.

Slowly I was gaining more insight into the question with which I continued to grapple, "Why me, a miracle?"

However, if I had known what lay ahead, that question would have had no importance, because I would have seriously considered bailing out on my commitment to God.

16
Strike the Tent

Why does it take so much work and sweat to lead someone into the kingdom of God?

I'm not talking about appeals to the cozy, comfy, snug whirrings of a mind trying to decide, "Shall I enter or shall I not?"

I'm talking about the "tent years" when we were nomads, roustabouts, stevedores, laborers, carpenters, musicians, cooks, singers and hospitality greeters first, and then we were evangelists.

We were no different in mobility than Ringling Brothers and Barnum & Bailey or any other circus or traveling tent show. We would move in, set up, conduct revival services, then strike the tent and move on.

Zeal arose out of my commitment to God when I was in Good Samaritan Hospital. I had no idea what was on the other side of tomorrow.

But this I knew. If there were a road marked with Burma Shave signs along the way, "Follow this yellow brick road to personal, financial and future security," I knew I would not be dancing down that path.

The sign on my path would point to "Eternal life," and it would lead me, at any cost, to anyone with eyes to see and ears to hear.

Several months after the prophecy in the wee hours of the morning in El Cajon, we three interns completed our evangelistic tour and returned to Portland.

I had met a very attractive young woman before I went to southern California, and although we had never dated, I thought about her quite a bit.

Her name was Greta Bonar. She pronounced her name, "Greeta." When she first started visiting our church, and later when Gordon or I would go out to Palmer Mill to hold services in the little schoolhouse, Greta would play the piano.

After I returned to Portland, we started dating. She was a tiny bit of a thing. She was outgoing, active and very articulate.

I was still shy. On the other hand I was caught up in the fervor of God's assignment. The most impressive things to me, in addition to how lovely she looked and how well she played the piano, were her genuine Christian commitments and our mutual interests.

After we dated for a while and discussed what we wanted in life, I found I couldn't fault her in any area. She simply wasn't flawed. I decided I wanted Greta to spend the rest of her life with me, and I asked her to do so.

She accepted, almost on the run. I was in a hurry, so rather than a long engagement or even an announcement, we eloped and were married on December 10, 1926.

A friend of ours by the name of West told us, "This marriage will last about six weeks." He felt Greta was too dainty and fragile for a rugged Canadian outdoorsman like me.

Well, I know West never went into the forecasting business, because Greta and I celebrated our golden wedding anniversary a number of years ago, and we're looking forward to many more anniversaries.

Greta may have been fragile, but she had the fiber, because one doesn't survive the vicissitudes of the Great Depression, our tent years, my evangelistic ministry and seven children unless one has the stuff to cope with raw adversity.

After our marriage we headed for Kingman in the province of Alberta, Canada, and I was soon preaching in the Lutheran church. Greta became acquainted with members of my family for the first time; I proudly showed her the area where I grew up.

I also investigated whether there was any inheritance from my father or uncle, to find there was none.

Before returning to Portland we moved to Edmonton, where I pastored a little church for about a year; our first son, Paul, was born there on November 6, 1927.

Greta and I moved back and settled down again in Portland. Gordon Lindsay and I resumed our close friendship as we continued preaching.

In 1928 a famous evangelist, Aimee Semple McPherson, was leading revival meetings in Portland. She had built a large church in Los Angeles in 1923, called the Angelus Temple.

She gained some unfair and unwarranted notoriety on the front pages of newspapers throughout America for five weeks in 1926, from May 18 to June 23. Some claimed she simply disappeared; the police accused her of hiding in northern California, producing alleged evidence to that effect, but later dropping all charges; she said she was kidnapped, and I believe that to be the case.

Gordon and I knew the strong faith of this woman and her very successful ministry and Pentecostal preaching in Los Angeles, because she was leading a tremendous revival of the Christian movement at the time we were conducting our tent services in El Cajon.

Greta, Gordon and I attended her revival in Portland. Crowds attended the services, and she led countless people into the kingdom of God. The prayer meetings were spiritually beautiful. There were many healings. Greta sang in the choir. Gordon and I were deeply moved by the revival and by Aimee when we met in fellowship with her after one of the services.

Our ministries were strengthened by the devout faith of Aimee Semple McPherson.

Not long thereafter, our second son, Floyd, was born in Portland on February 11, 1929.

Greta and I were getting itchy; we felt we'd spent enough time in the headwaters in Alberta and Oregon, and we were now ready for the evangelistic mainstream. But this was not to be, yet.

Greta's mother, Maude Mabel Bonar, had become ill with cancer, so we delayed our departure. I continued to preach, while Greta, now pregnant, nursed her mother.

Our first daughter, Maybelle, was born on September 7, 1930. But sadness soon followed this joy, when Greta's mother died in March of 1931.

Soon after that, we packed our worldly belongings, loaded them in our car, and the five Welches motored south on the narrow and sometimes unpaved highway down through Oregon and California to Arizona.

We located a tent and started our revival meetings through Arizona. We moved to several towns and then drove into Douglas and set up our "big top."

I conducted one service. Later that night a fierce windstorm arose, blowing our tent across the Mexican border toward Agua Prieta. We searched and searched, but we never did find that tent.

This was only the beginning of the real tent years. We hauled the tents ourselves from one town to another; we pulled them on trailers behind our cars. We put them up; we took them down. We manhandled the heavy canvas.

We set up chairs; we took them down. We hoisted a sign; we took it down. We unfolded Greta's portable organ; we folded it away again. We assembled an altar and a pulpit; we disassembled them.

We improvised. If we didn't have it, we invented it.

When the weather was kind, it was very kind, but when it was bad, it was very bad. Tents blew down on us; they blew away from us. We survived rainstorms, windstorms, sleet, ice and devastating heat. Weather eventually took its toll, tearing and ripping the canvas. Greta sewed canvas until her fingers were bloody.

To keep the revival moving, untold people helped us.

And God was with us all the time, or we couldn't have done it.

We finished our tent revivals in Arizona and decided our next destination would be Louisiana. The Welches began a long trip over a narrow ribbon of road through New Mexico, across Texas to Fort Worth and Dallas, and then on to Olla, Louisiana.

Later we visited some friends in Shreveport. I held a revival meeting there while I was a guest of Jack Moore, whose father-in-law pastored an Assembly of God church.

We returned to Olla, in the heart of Huey Long country. Gordon Lindsay joined us at this time, and we proceeded to hold some of the most anointed "fire and brimstone" tent revival services ever held in the Bible Belt, in Olla and Winnfield.

These were oil towns, inhabited by men with the brawn and muscle to match the rigors of drilling and wildcatting. They were not afraid of anything or anybody.

Along with that bravado came some parched hearts and souls, too. They wanted an infilling of spiritual love and faith as much as anyone, perhaps a little more so. In any event, many of them gave their lives to God.

Everyone of us had to help, no matter the shifting circumstances.

Gordon and I registered for a conference in Mississippi. There was no one else to preach the gospel for the three days we'd be gone, except Greta.

Gordon and I sat down with her and boosted her confidence, telling her, "You can do it. You know the

Scriptures. And you've heard us so many times, you know the service by heart. And you lead the singing anyway. God won't let you fail. You can do it."

And she did. While we were away, she took care of our three children, prepared the tent, played the organ, led the singing of the hymns and preached the sermon.

Little Greta was cast in among those towering oil men to talk to them about their eternal lives. And Greta led them to God.

In 1932 the Welches moved to Laurel, Mississippi, where I conducted a revival for Pastor Noel at his First Assembly of God church.

From there we piled everything into the car and drove to Atlanta, Georgia, where I helped Pastor Shaw conduct services in another big tent revival.

As it turned out, we stayed a little longer than we had planned, because Shaw's daughter, who played the piano for the revival, was going to have a baby. We revised our timetable so we could remain another two weeks; Greta played the piano, and I continued to help with the prayer meetings.

Another stop on the Welch circuit was Greenville, South Carolina, where we met the death plague of the 1930s.

Our host, Pastor Clevenger, was conducting a revival, when he suddenly developed black diphtheria. A quarantine sign was posted on the front door of his home; there was no one to take care of him, except me.

So I served his food in separate dishes, to avoid contagion, and nursed him as best I could. In addition, I assumed his duties in his church; I was preaching every night.

It was not long before I developed scabs in my throat. They turned black. I prayed, "Lord, I've got too much to do. I can't come down with diphtheria. In your name I'm going to continue."

I took the kid's sucker sticks and wrapped cotton around them to fashion a swab. I'll admit they didn't look as professional as a swab from Johnson and Johnson, but the swab from Welch and Welch did the job. And, in the depth of the Depression, the price was right.

I dipped the swab's cotton in peroxide and applied my medication to the black masses in my throat.

As sick as I was, I continued to preach every night, until Clevenger himself arose from his sick bed as a well man to return to his pulpit. My Physician had healed me, too.

After I attended a convention in Kentucky, I returned to Greenville. We loaded the car once again with bag and baggage and moved to Waynesboro, Mississippi.

Shortly after I settled down, a black Methodist pastor asked me to preach in his church. I agreed readily, "Sure."

However, after word spread quickly on the grapevine what I intended to do, I was approached by a white man, who informed me he couldn't believe I'd agreed to preach in the black man's church. He said, "This just isn't done. It's never been done."

Then he asked me point-blank, "Are you going to preach to them?"

"Yes, they've got a soul, too, you know," I responded. And one Sunday I did preach proudly in that black pastor's church, because we were both men of God. I just told his congregation about Jesus Christ.

This happened to me again on a trip to Alabama. We invited everyone to our revival meetings, and for us, that included black Christians.

The owner of a country store was enraged and told me I had no business inviting those people to our services. I responded in the only way I knew how, "You know, the gospel is for everyone. If God is for the bootleggers and rumrunners and whiskey kings out here in these bottoms, why won't He do something for everyone?"

The man was not happy with my answer. He stomped off.

In all, there were about ten of us in our twenties holding these revival meetings. Gordon Lindsay and I called everyone together and discussed the impending crisis.

We finally agreed to set up a special side for the "colored people." To my knowledge there wasn't such an arrangement in any of the churches or revival meetings being held at this time.

In Waynesboro our church was a theater that had long since gone out of business. We didn't pay anything for the theater, other than our agreement to maintain the building. I suppose we were among the first to launch what would later be called "storefront churches," although our necessity grew out of Depression desperation.

In many towns our tents and those empty buildings were all we had for a place of worship.

One night a tall, Lincolnesque man sauntered into our

Waynesboro service and sat down in the back. I didn't pay much attention to him other than notice him enter, but God spoke to me as I was conducting the service to go back and minister to this man.

Wow! What a story about the power of God! In talking with him after the prayer meeting, I found out this was Will Purvis, the same man we had read about in the newspapers. His story started with an amazing incident and continued over many years, later to be made famous nationally in the *Reader's Digest*.

It started when Will was a very young man. An ambush party shot and killed a man, Will Buckley, in Columbia, Mississippi, in 1893, before he could testify and name names to a grand jury, as he claimed he would.

An eyewitness escaped the assassins, according to his account; the eyewitness, the brother of Will Buckley, fingered Will Purvis, testifying he was responsible for the murder of his brother.

Notwithstanding the testimony of five neighbors and friends that Will Purvis could not have committed the crime because they saw him at home at the time, and notwithstanding evidence that Will's shotgun had not been fired for months, nevertheless, the jury voted a verdict of guilty. The sentence: death, by hanging.

The pastor of Columbia Methodist Church, Reverend W.S. Sibley, visited Will in jail, became convinced of his innocence, introduced him to Jesus Christ, whom he accepted as his Savior to enter the kingdom of God, and then convened a weekly prayer meeting to appeal to God that this innocent man be spared from death on the gallows.

The day of execution arrived. Almost three thousand people gathered at the Marion county courthouse square to witness the hanging.

The experienced executioners, the sheriff and his deputies, tested the rope and the trap door; both were ready. They tied together the hands and feet of Will Purvis.

Before positioning the black hood over his face, the officers turned to Reverend Sibley.

Standing next to Will, he offered a simple, thirteen-word supplication, talking only to God, but with a hushed crowd leaning forward to eavesdrop, "Almighty God, if it be thy will, stay the hand of the executioner." That's all he said.

The hood was positioned.

The trap was sprung.

The crowd gasped. The body shot toward the open trap door.

The body shot *through* the open trap door. It didn't jerk to a stop; it didn't dangle; it didn't twist in the wind.

The noose uncoiled its deadly, choking grip; the rope swung free, and where it once held Will's neck, it now held only air. God had stayed the hand of the executioner!

The officers dragged him to the top of the platform to hang him again. But the miracle had changed the minds of the people and, soon also, the resolve of the executioners. They returned Will to jail.

Several appeals were made to the governor and the Supreme Court to remove Will from death row, but their pleas were to no avail.

A group of outraged vigilantes, now convinced of Will's innocence, and impatient with justice seemingly deaf to their appeals, took the law into their own hands and freed Will from jail.

In spite of a reward offered by the governor, no one apprehended him. A new governor was elected; one of his campaign promises was to commute the death sentence of Purvis to life imprisonment, which he did.

Later Will received a full pardon and married the daughter of a Baptist minister.

And a number of years later, an old planter, Joe Beard, confessed on his deathbed that he and another man committed the crime for which Purvis had been convicted. Purvis was now forty-seven.

The Mississippi legislature paid Will Purvis $5,000 to atone for the grievous injustice, for "hanging" an innocent man.

After talking with Will in the back of the church, a spiritual camaraderie grew out of our similar experiences of being blessed by God with extraordinary miracles in our lives.

He told me he had been faithful in his Christian walk, but recently he had wandered away and wanted to renew his commitment to God; that's why he was here.

I prayed with him right there until the early hours of the next morning when he reconsecrated his life to God. There are no moments more beautiful than when two men are praying on their knees for many hours in the presence of God.

After a year in Waynesboro I moved my family to

Meridian, Mississippi, where we were to be blessed by two more children. Madeira was born on June 24, 1934, and James, August 21, 1935.

Even among lean years these were the leanest. We had everything we needed except money. I would be reminded of our stark existence many years later when Humphrey Bogart, terminally ill with cancer, was reported in the press to have said, "All we've got is money."

But in the nadir of the Depression there was no money; people couldn't go anywhere but to church or our revivals. They loved to sing. So when we set up on high school campuses or in tents or buildings, Greta brought along her little folding organ and started playing thirty minutes before we began our services; some young musicians traveled with us and played along with Greta. This music really attracted the crowds.

The Welches remained on the move, even though we established homes for short periods of time in some of the towns we visited. The next town we called home was Louisville, Mississippi, where Marilyn was born July 6, 1937.

Wherever we went, our six children accompanied us. When people asked Greta how in the world she raised so many young babies and growing tykes in the nomadic life we lived, she always responded with a chuckle, "They've all been brought up on the front seat of the church."

Along with everyone else, the Welch family had faced all the hardships, dangers, diseases and privations the times had to offer, except one, indigenous to the South, but we were not to be overlooked for long.

Soon we would find ourselves helpless in the path of the onslaught of a roaring killer tornado.

17
"A Tornado's Out There"

Summer. 1937. The scratching years of the Great Depression were behind us. And with us. And ahead of us.

How long could these magnificent people of the South endure such suffering of poverty? Not a poverty of wants, nor a poverty of luxuries, but a poverty of needs.

Of all those who came to me for comfort, in their eyes I saw the ravages of years of scratching and, deep inside, lonely, resigned sobbing. I sustained them only because my comfort was not mine, but His that sent me.

A feeling nudged me that I was needed elsewhere. I sat down and shared it with my wife.

"I'm not happy here. I'm not doing all I can for God. I'd like to pastor another church, Greta, maybe build one, somewhere.

"You know, I've heard a lot about Wheeler up in the Twenty-Mile Bottom country. Five revenue officers just disappeared there, not long ago.

"I think I'll go up to Wheeler and look around and see

if there's room for the eight of us up there. The people in that moonshine country better repent and come to God, with what's going on in that bottom land.

"I guess I'd better get my tie and Sunday clothes. You know, it's strange, Greta, but it's true—some people think if you don't look holy, you aren't."

I hopped in my Chevrolet and headed north, churning up clouds of dust behind me for 120 miles on a steamy August Saturday afternoon.

The buildings in Wheeler were all boarded up except a few, and one of these was the country store, where I parked. Once inside, I walked up to a man who gave every indication he owned the store, and he did. I introduced myself and learned he was Martin Franks.

"Mr. Franks, I'd like to hold a revival in Wheeler. With some of the buildings not in use around here, I'm wondering if one's available."

Four men around him grimaced and looked me up and down. They heard what I said. There was no mistaking the expressions on their faces, "A revival?"

Frank stared at me and flipped three silver dollars he palmed in his right hand. This feudal baron who owned Wheeler measured the Scripture, "Prove all things," against me; he threw down the gauntlet.

"Well, there are about one hundred people close by in town. Why don't you just preach to us today? Right now."

I looked at the henchmen around him, undoubtedly some of the toughest bootleggers who had ever walked. They weren't menacing or threatening me, but they weren't in agreement with what I had in mind, either.

"We've never had a preacher in this place," continued Franks. "I built the Baptist church here, but I don't call that preaching. Nobody goes but me and my family."

I didn't say anything. I just looked out through the front door onto the dirt street while I listened to the Holy Spirit.

Finally I responded to Franks, "Well, if you want me to preach the Word right now, we'll have to go outside."

I walked over to a railroad boxcar on a spur next to his country store. The boxcar was empty, and there was nothing in front of it. I could talk to a crowd of people here and they could easily see me and hear me.

I took my Bible and climbed up into the open door. I just stood there for a moment and looked around. With Franks and his friends prominently in attendance, people knew something was going to happen. The town folk started gathering.

The weather was hot and muggy. I looked at the buildings with their windows and doors all boarded up. These were not old buildings awaiting demolition; take off the boards and they were ready for business and commerce, but there was precious little of that.

I looked at the people as they gathered, and in a sense they were boarded up, too, their hopes and dreams and aspirations.

Their clothing was threadbare, with patches; the very fabric of Wheeler.

The heat was oppressive. Poverty was oppressive.

But I could see these were sturdy, gallant, spiritually hungry people. As I looked into their eyes, the feeling of the Holy Spirit swept over me.

I just started to preach. On judgment. And the lake of fire. I was really inspired.

And I knew the source of the inspiration. The assembly of people was so quiet I could hear my voice bounce off the empty buildings and ricochet down the street.

If a bird were looking down, this must be quite a scene: a fiery Bible-belt evangelist, with the Scriptures in one hand and gesturing with the other, framed in an open door of a railroad boxcar, in the center of town, delivering an impromptu sermon, to an impromptu gathering, under a searing Southern sun, in the depths of the Great Depression.

After I finished, I jumped down from the boxcar and made my way to Franks, not knowing what to expect.

I heard the thump-chink, thump-chink, thump-chink of the three silver dollars.

Without missing a beat, he delivered his pronouncement, "Any open building in this town you want, it's yours, if you'll move here and stay with us for a while.

"The ministry is so weak around here they couldn't cast the devil out of a peanut.

"You don't know it, but we need what you've got to preach. We'll seat them. We'll provide anything you need."

Franks had spoken and, though he didn't know it, God had spoken, too. The Welches embarked on a new life in Wheeler.

Over the next several years countless hundreds of people in the Twenty-Mile Bottom country and beyond

106

were led to God and baptized in water.

It seemed almost every bootlegger, rumrunner and whiskey king came forward to God for salvation, with one notable exception.

He noised it around that not only would he not attend our services, he wouldn't let his wife attend either.

Sometimes she would sneak out and come to church. He'd come storming right into church in the middle of my service and yank her out. He was a mean man.

I didn't know it then, but it would not be long before he would be the victim of a horrible tragedy.

These were glorious years. There was a great sweep of souls coming into the kingdom of God in Mississippi and throughout the South, and particularly in our home church in Wheeler. I had never been busier, conducting revivals in tents and churches in Alabama, Tennessee, Kentucky, South Carolina, Arkansas, Georgia and Louisiana.

I'd attend a prayer meeting anywhere, anytime.

And I couldn't be happier with the services in our little storefront church in Wheeler. The converted store was comfortable and the price was right; the only financial responsibilities were maintenance and utilities.

However, our congregation had been growing over the several years since we started the church. Almost every Sunday now, latecomers had a choice of standing or leaving. And to me, that was no choice at all; I was here to introduce people to the kingdom of God, not turn them away.

Finally, one week I visited with Franks and other community leaders and discussed my plans for a new church building just outside of town. Everyone was in accord, if church members and I would be the architects, contractors and labor. We would.

On a knoll south of town we started building our Wheeler Tabernacle. It would seat three hundred, more than three times the congregation which attended my first impromptu sermon several years ago.

We poured a foundation of concrete about ten inches in width around the outer perimeter of the building. With almost no funds, and building materials that would go just so far, we skipped lumber in favor of a sawdust floor.

I worked like no man has ever worked to construct our new house of God. We painted the building and the steeple white, and the cross on the steeple. I thought to myself, "It's not unlike the Canadian church in Kingman, is it?"

After it was finished, all of those who labored so hard during construction rejoiced; it was magnificent and solid as a rock. We built that Tabernacle so sound it would take a Judgment Day storm to destroy it. At least, we thought so.

Not long after we completed the Tabernacle, a neighbor came running into my house, not far from the church, yelling, "Reverend Welch! Reverend Welch! A tornado's out there."

I dashed outside to locate it. Sure enough, there it was, coming right up "Tornado Alley." The twister had hit and torn apart Baldwyn to the south, then vectored six miles up the railroad tracks toward Wheeler.

These were the same tracks on the Baldwyn-Wheeler line where Jimmie Rodgers saw a water tank and got the idea for a country song, with lyrics to express the scene, "Sitting by a water tank waiting for a train."

His sister and some of his friends, who were musicians, had attended our services in Waynesboro. This was while Rodgers was very ill with tuberculosis, before he died in 1933. He and his talent were respected highly in this part of the South. When he was elected to the Country Music Hall of Fame in 1961, Jimmie Rodgers was credited "in the country music field as the one who started it all."

As for Baldwyn, I had preached on the main street many times. I preached judgment, "Repent, or God will send something along to wipe you out." I was thinking of a tornado which had struck not far away a few years before. I warned, "Remember what He did to Tupelo."

I looked at the funnel rising five thousand feet into the air.

Half of the town of Baldwyn must be in it! The twister appeared to be moving in slow motion, with the lower portion of the funnel swaying drunkenly off balance to the right and to the left.

It was coming toward us at a speed of about six miles an hour.

I took the seven members of my family to the southern wall of the Tabernacle. I calmed them as much as I could and told them to lie down along the concrete foundation facing the path of the tornado.

"That wall will protect you. It's solid concrete anchored in the ground.

"If anything blows away here, if it does take out that foundation, and there's nothing stronger than that, it's goodbye anyway."

Little Maybelle followed my instructions but then noticed I was still standing and about to leave. She looked up at me, "Daddy, where are you going?"

I then told my family, "I'm going outside and talk to God."

On my way there I could see people scrambling into storm cellars which had been dug into the bank beneath the railway tracks.

I stood on the knoll and surveyed the tornado, as it growled a steady, threatening roar. The funnel menaced the Tabernacle, Wheeler, our home and me.

While this was not a Judgment Day storm, I was forced to admit the Tabernacle was no match for this raging cyclone.

I was by myself now, alone. I looked up and raised my hands, outstretched, in prayer.

"God, I'm going to be like Moses. You've listened to me preach faith and you've listened to me preach your power to these people.

"God, I'm going to stand here in your name. If everything is going to be blown away, I'm going to be blown away, too, if that's what you want."

I stood there. Silently. My eyes and hands lifted up to God. Slowly the tornado stopped. Right down there in the bottom of the valley, now no more than half a mile away.

Caught up in this towering struggle between supreme forces, I looked out there and shouted, "Devil, you're the prince of the power of the air, and I command you in the name of Jesus not to come any closer to me than this.

"You stay right where you are, because you're not hurting anyone or anything down there in that cotton field."

The funnel hovered there for what seemed to be an eternity. I remained where I was, heels firmly planted, silently, with my eyes and hands raised once again in prayer to God.

The people in the storm bunkers peered out of their holes, looked at me silhouetted on the knoll against ominous black clouds and shook their heads.

They could not comprehend anyone foolish enough to meet a tornado head on. Sure, I had preached the power of faith; however, this was going a little too far.

But this was much more than a Sunday school exemplification of faith, and much more than any pastor's homily on faith, *this was faith.*

I stood there. And the funnel hovered in the cotton field.

Finally, I rebuked the threat again, "Devil, you want to tear all this up, to shatter the faith that I have preached to all these people. In the name of Jesus Christ, you're not going to do it."

Slowly the tornado started moving to the left, almost perpendicular to the railroad tracks. It continued its destructive march to the east.

Unfortunately, the twister bore down on the lonely man's property. He was the single vocal dissenter who fought us all the time and didn't want his wife attending church.

Three quarters of a mile from his house, they found

him dead, wrapped around a sapling with almost every bone in his body broken.

His home was scattered over the countryside. His chickens and cows were destroyed.

His loyal wife accompanied him into the eye of the tornado, but she came through, except for a broken leg, unscathed. Her injury hobbled her for a while, but she survived and recovered.

When it was all over, rain drenched down for half an hour, the water ran off, the sun broke through, and our Tabernacle and little town of Wheeler were saved.

The nation now believed what the radio had been saying time and again, "Prosperity is just around the corner." Also around the corner were some world-churning events foretold in the prophetic words at El Cajon.

18
"Branham's Coming"

Shortly after the Japanese attacked Pearl Harbor, December 7, 1941, I joined the war effort, as we moved to Memphis, Tennessee.

However, one more Welch had just joined us; Mary Ann was born October 6 in Wheeler. As I looked down where Greta said we reared our children, on the front pew of the church, I now saw proudly what would be our completed family, four daughters and three sons.

In Memphis I was busier than ever with three demanding responsibilities.

Lockheed sent me as a student to the Shelby County School of Aeronautics. We were placed in training on the electrical and mechanical systems of the P-41, P-48 and P-51. In time, some captured Japanese Zeros were shipped to us for detailed examination to determine the strengths and weaknesses of their system components and operations and the possible existence of any secret equipment. All we found was technology inferior to ours, but not inferior in terms of a platform for launching death and destruction to our fighting men at the front.

At the same time I was employed by Tri-State Electric Company. Tri-State was under contract with the Navy for development of landing craft. Another man and I designed the pilot model wiring panel for these landing craft, which would later be used in the South Pacific.

In addition, I continued to preach in churches, tents or wherever there was a handful of people who wanted to hold a revival or a prayer meeting.

Meantime, we received a telegram that Greta's father, James Bonar, had died. Greta and Mary Ann departed immediately by Greyhound bus for what turned out to be an extended stay in Portland.

After a few months of hyperactivity for me in Memphis, expecially adding the duty of parenting alone all our youngsters except Mary Ann, I decided to load the car once again with belongings, bundles, luggage and Welches and embark for Portland. We drove into Portland December 27, 1942.

During the remainder of World War II, I ministered in a small church, the Church of God, and helped the war effort working on a production line as supervisor of a crew of men manufacturing axles for trucks and trailers for the Army.

With the surrender of the Japanese, and V-J Day August 15, 1945, thus ended the second epoch event foretold to us in prophetic words by God in El Cajon.

In the face of a protracted global war, there was an ebb in the fervor of Christian faith.

There may have been some new "foxhole Christians,"

as we were told, but if so, as far as I could determine, those who didn't die in their foxholes crawled out and left their new faith exactly where they found it, not unlike others in life, saying in effect, "God, I *almost* needed You back there."

Christianity on the home front was no better. There was no wartime or postwar groundswell of faith or living, dynamic manifestations of gifts of the Spirit or fruit of the Spirit, and there was little church or evangelistic leadership.

A spiritual drought settled over the country; things really got dry. In fact, church work was so dead that all it needed was a funeral and someone to throw some dirt in on it and to give it a benediction. And I say that, lamentably, as an active pastor.

After the war, the three of us who started out as green, evangelistic interns gravitated together again, Gordon Lindsay, Leon Hall and me.

In 1947 Gordon wired me from Shreveport, Louisiana, "Tom, what God told us in 1926 has come to pass." He was referring to that portion of the prophecy in which God said, after a drought in the gifts of the Spirit, there would be a restoration and a great outpouring of the gifts, especially the gift of Healing, and if we were faithful, we would live to see it and have a part in it.

Gordon asked if I would reserve the Civic Auditorium in Portland and organize a real jumping off place for an evangelist he met recently.

Gordon had attended a healing service one evening in a church in Sacramento conducted by a William Branham, a former game warden and a Baptist minister from Jeffersonville, Indiana.

Gordon was deeply impressed and spiritually inspired, seeing the evangelist call forth deaf mutes and the blind to pray for their healings, when Gordon witnessed those healings himself.

At the conclusion of the long prayer meeting, he saw Reverend Branham walk toward some steps to leave, when the evangelist happened to turn back to see a little cross-eyed girl sitting to one side; she, perhaps like others, had not had the courage to go forward.

He returned, took her to him, put his hands over her eyes and prayed a brief prayer. When he removed his hands and the child looked up, she looked at him with eyes that had been straightened, now perfectly normal. She was the last one he prayed for that night.

Gordon told me these miracles happened wherever Branham went, and he was willing to go anywhere to minister to the sick. He illustrated with another miraculous healing. Branham visited a woman in her home, dying of tuberculosis. In fact, she was in her last hours. Gordon related that one man who saw her said she was so thin from her sickness that you could hold a flashlight to her backbone and look right through her. There was nothing left of her.

Branham prayed for her and commanded her in the name of Jesus, "Rise, take up thy bed, and walk, and accept your healing."

She did. She got up and walked. She stayed up. And in time, she returned to her normal weight. She was healed.

"Tom, this man's got the gift," Gordon enthused, "it's just flowing and flowing and following him all the time, but he's been cooped up in small churches. All they seem to want to do is keep him inside four little walls because it'll make their organizations grow."

I understood what Gordon was saying, because by this time, I'd had extensive experience with all denominations of churches, including a few of my own.

I knew Gordon so well I neither questioned him nor doubted that William Branham was chosen by God for miracles.

We had been told in El Cajon this was coming. Of course, I was ready.

I scheduled the Civic Auditorium for three nights just after November 11 and immediately visited the offices of the Portland *Oregonian* to place the first newspaper advertising notice.

When they asked me what we wanted to say in the notice, I told them, "Branham's Coming." That's all I wanted to say.

The people in the newspaper office raised an eyebrow at my not putting in the time and place and other promotional details. "That's not very much."

"No, it isn't," I responded, "but that's all we want to say now. In two weeks we want to include some more information."

The audiences got progressively larger; on the final night the auditorium was packed with a great congregation, including scores of ministers.

Many miracles of healing took place during the revival,

with a multitude of people ministered to in the prayer line.

Gordon was right; Branham had the gift. He was filled with the Holy Spirit and led many in Portland into the kingdom of God. But his ministry was healing; the power of God simply flowed through the man.

Branham was humble, meek and unassuming. He told me, "Tom, I'm not a learned man. My power of healing is not mine; I'm helpless until I feel His presence. God heals the sick, I don't. God performs the miracles, I don't. There have been thousands of healings, of all kinds of diseases. I have been told that if I'm sincere and persuade people to believe, nothing will stand before my prayer, not even cancer.

"Tom, I don't know how much longer God will grant me His almighty power in my healing ministry. I'm trying to do what I've been told to do the best I can, but I need help. No mortal can take credit for performing a miracle, and I'm just a mortal. I myself don't know how to do anything."

Evangelists and ministers are sometimes willing to be promoted into big-name, superstar idols, but not William Branham; he was a true disciple of the Lord God. His ministry grew, prospered and flourished all over the country.

Over the years I was blessed to find my path crossing those of evangelists and ministers who were devout men and women of God; sadly, a few faltered.

On the national scene I had met, witnessed or participated in fellowship with a few who received some

118

prominence and recognition.

One of those was Billy Sunday, who visited Portland in 1925. He conducted a revival at the official opening of a new tabernacle, seating thousands, in downtown Portland, close to the Multnomah Athletic Club. I attended all of his services over several days; each time the tabernacle was filled. He was a no-nonsense man of faith, fascinating and impressive. He laced his sermons with colorful baseball language; he had played for the Chicago White Sox. He was a sin-blasting preacher.

"I don't have the home-run hitting ministry Dr. Price has received from the Lord, but I know we're going on to new and greater things, so I'm going to take my turns at bat with what God's called me to do." That was Billy Sunday's introduction to our next evangelist at the tabernacle that fall.

Dr. Charles Price was a well-regarded, well-known pastor from Lodi, California, who had become an evangelist as a result of a humbling fall. He explained the incident in services I attended.

He went to Aimee Semple McPherson's campaign in Lodi with one purpose in mind: to debunk tongues, interpretations and all those ridiculous things practiced by Evangelist McPherson.

He sat up front with a group from his congregation in a defiant, heckling frame of mind. During the service she turned to him as the congregation was standing; Dr. Price said a few simple, prayerful words, at which the evangelist stretched out her hand toward him and spoke directly to Dr. Price; without warning, he fell under the power of God, collapsed and found himself lying flat on his back in the sawdust.

"When I got up," he smiled, "I felt like a disgraceful rag doll, rather than the ramrod straight pastor of a large church in Lodi, and I had learned something about the power of God in the ministry of Aimee Semple McPherson and her frivolous, ceremonial rubbish. I soon left my pastorship to become an evangelist, emulating you-know-who."

In 1948 I was in Los Angeles and attended a service of a young, emerging, firebrand evangelist, Billy Graham. There was no mistaking the power of God in his life.

His revivals have been very consistent over the years. In 1948 he delivered a sermon ending with an evangelistic call for those in the audience to come forward and give their hearts to God. Countless people went forward; it was a beautiful moment of prayer.

He has led an exemplary life, passing up an opportunity as a handsome young man to become, perhaps, a movie star in Hollywood. What a loss that would have been to the Christian world.

Billy Graham has certainly been the most famous of all the evangelists during the many years of his ministry and has undoubtedly been responsible for a tremendous momentum in the interdenominational, ecumenical movement throughout the world.

Another Christian leader was Dr. John G. Lake, who shaped my ministry from the very beginning, as I've mentioned. He trained me for the clergy in his church in Portland. As Gordon Lindsay wrote on the title page of a book of Dr. Lake's sermons, his "healing ministry in missionary fields was considered the greatest of his generation."

My close colleague, Gordon Lindsay, was very active in God's work. He was a minister who guided many evangelists on tours and campaigns in a sweeping revival of Christian faith and gifts of the Spirit.

Gordon and his wife, Freda, were co-founders of Christ For The Nations, Inc., a missionary organization which has helped to build 5,500 churches in 118 nations. Gordon launched Voice of Healing magazine in 1948 and wrote 250 books. He and Freda, a dear friend of ours, were pioneer publishers of Christian literature. They founded a Christian publishing house, now in Dallas, Texas. Gordon has been sorely missed in the years since his death in 1973.

For a number of years after World War II, Gordon and I discussed the need for an organization of full gospel churches and ministers. There were many independent churches around the country and the world which would benefit from an interchange of spiritual love and fellowship.

We did not want it to become in any way a governing body. Neither did we foresee the need for an organization to license or ordain ministers. Rather, we visualized a concept of a structure simply to provide expression for the essential unity of the body of Christ under the leadership of the Holy Spirit, a unity that goes beyond individuals, churches or organizations.

In 1955 initial drafts of bylaws to be incorporated into a constitution were completed. The Fellowship was launched officially in 1957.

By 1980 the Full Gospel Fellowship of Churches and Ministers International was composed of 600 churches and 1,000 ministers, whose existence for being has been stated: for the unity of the body of Christ and the sovereignty of the local church. In 1980 I continued my active participation as executive vice-president of the northwest region.

Over the years, sadly, I have also brushed against ministers who have faltered and no longer believe. One concealed his evil until it exploded on the international scene.

In the early 1950s I was in Oakland when a friend of mine invited me to attend a prayer meeting in a large theater, to be conducted by Reverend Jim Jones. Even though I had strong feelings which led me to tell my friend, "God does not approve of this ministry," they were not so strong in discernment as to provide an inkling that this fundamentalist preacher would mesmerize 900 people into taking their own lives, along with him, in November, 1978, in Guyana.

All this was after Jones established his church, "People's Temple," in San Francisco, became a political leader in the Bay Area, promoted himself, stomped on the Bible in his services and gathered innocent people into his ugly, evil cult, slowly spinning a web from which few followers would escape, all in the name, at least initially, of the Lord.

The Lord had told me in the hospital I should not be surprised that worldly shackles abound, sought eagerly by the free; and of all worldly relationships we should abide in Him above all: first, last and always.

There was another man who was one of the greatest evangelists ever to cross this country.

Gordon and Leon and I started him on his way. He had the rawest faith of any evangelist in modern times. He came from nowhere with nothing. He didn't even have any presentable clothes in which to preach, and he had an old car that would look more at home on the junk heap than on the street.

He could lay his hands on anything and it would just turn over. That was where the miracles were happening, with him. God had chosen him and endowed him with a powerful gift of healing. He conducted some of the greatest revivals around the country.

All of this happened in postwar years. The evangelist achieved fame, money, attention and adulation, all that mankind can bestow, too.

Sadly, he succumbed to immoral misconduct, the same immorality he solemnly preached against.

Suddenly, he lost his power from the source. God withdrew His power. I wish those things affected only the person involved, but they do not. It affected me as much as it affected him.

Later, with no condemnation and with abundant forgiveness, we tried to help this evangelist get started again. Gordon and Leon and I combined to give him our support. I went up to Spokane, Washington, as advance man, arranged for the Masonic Temple and prepared the necessary arrangements.

He preached three nights in Spokane. I left early for Pasco to prepare for his revivals in the tri-city area. All the arrangements were completed; we were set for his arrival. But, he never arrived.

In the last afternoon in Spokane, just before he was scheduled to depart to join me, he dropped exhausted into a chair. Spiritual joy was drained from his face.

He turned to our colleagues and said, "I want to thank everyone for your help and kindness in setting up this tour.

"But I just don't have the anointing anymore. The power of God is not flowing as it has before. I'm canceling the remainder of the campaign.

"I'm not going to preach again."

The taste of rebuke can be bitter, indeed.

Beginning late in the 1940s, for a decade it seemed everybody we prayed for was healed.

But then a great spiritual drought settled over the land. As God had told us in the prophecy, the love of money and power became the consuming drive for most Americans. And the reckless gratification of esteem, self, sexual appetites—all the pleasures of the senses.

The times of holy drought would continue until the latter part of the 1970s.

Some ministries produced fruit. Healings continued as the gifts of the Spirit flowed through those chosen by God.

The prophecy had been accurate, too, as it pertained to some believers, "They that believe, will believe no more."

Sadly, this ran the spectrum from clergy to laity, and

the trend continues.

But the awakening, the outpouring, the renaissance, has begun.

When the Lord talked to me in my hospital bed about the free will of mankind, I learned well, but not well enough. Later I would be given empirical teaching which I would never forget.

19
Holy Right: Free to Choose

Why is it that each of us, at times, must go to school on experience?

As a child, "Don't touch the burning cinder" is only so much grouch until it turns into ouch.

Jesus, in His patience with me in my room at Good Samaritan, articulated the holy concept and crucial meaning of man's free will.

I understood. And I observed it, as a scientist in a laboratory, in my evangelistic work over many years, but I, too, would pick up the burning cinder, not once, but twice.

However, not out of defiance. Out of love.

Orville Ross and I were sitting in his home in Oakland engaged in discussion; I was there to conduct a revival in the church of a friend of mine. It was 1948.

With a great rush, his daughter ran into the house with tears in her eyes and yelled, "Dad, come quick, grandmother's dead."

Orville grabbed his coat; as his arms found the sleeves

on the way to the door, he trailed over his shoulder, "Tom, I'm going to run on over there. You're welcome to come, if you want." And Orville was gone.

His mother-in-law lived only a few blocks away. I walked over to see if there was anything I could do.

As I entered, Orville and his wife gave me the news, "She's had a heart attack, Tom. She's dead. The ambulance is on the way."

Sitting in a rocking chair, she was slumped to one side. Her head hung down motionless, with a pink, frothy foam issuing out of her mouth and down her blouse.

I can't tell you why, but I walked to the back of her chair; I reached around and, with a prayer for life in the name of the Lord, I lifted her head and held it high for a moment.

She opened her eyes. She looked at me.

The ambulance arrived. Orville came out of his chair at the surprising turn of events.

The ambulance attendants rushed in. "Looks like she's alive. What happened?"

"I just came in the door," I responded, "and walked around here and lifted up her chin in the name of the Lord and here she is, alive."

The attendants placed her on a stretcher, loaded her carefully in the ambulance and sped off to the hospital.

She never spoke a word.

Orville and his wife rode in the ambulance with her. On the way, she turned to them, and said, "Why did Brother Welch do that?

"Why did he pray for me? I didn't want to come back. I

was happy. I didn't want to return."

She stayed in the Oakland hospital overnight. They brought her home the next day.

She then related why she didn't want to come back, "I'd gone on to heaven. Everything was beautiful, wonderful. Friends met me; I was with people I knew. I was very happy where I was."

In six months she continued her journey to be where she wanted to be, of her own free will. One day the Rosses found her dead.

She never recanted in her remaining months; nor did she ever forgive me for what she firmly believed I did, entreat the power of the Lord to bring her back to life.

In 1964, one day I got a phone call from Allie Swartz in Portland. She gave me the latest report on her husband in the hospital in Hillsboro, not good.

Carl had a brain hemorrhage and was in intensive care, unconscious, not expected to live.

"Tom, will you go over and pray for him? I don't want to lose him, Tom, and I'm afraid I will, unless you pray for a healing.

"The doctors say he has almost no chance of pulling through this. My only hope is you, Tom, and your prayers." I told Allie when I'd be at the hospital.

I thought she would meet me there, but when I arrived, she was nowhere to be found. I was directed to Carl's room in intensive care.

I walked in and stood beside his bed. I spoke to him. There was no response.

All at once I felt a strong infusion of the Holy Spirit.

Without any question, I felt the immense power of healing available to my faith in prayer for Carl.

I laid my hand on Carl's forehead, closed my eyes and opened my mouth to pray for the Lord God to raise him up from his sick bed in complete healing, when my prayer was interrupted before it began. I felt the soft pressure of what seemed to be a giant, unseen hand on my chest, gently pushing me away from Carl to the end of the bed.

I found myself at his feet, looking at him, the length of the bed.

I was perplexed. I didn't understand. I knew this strange, supernatural phenomenon was only a prelude, but to what?

After a moment, God spoke to me, "You've got faith to pray for a healing, and I'll heal him. But if I touch him, are you willing to be responsible for him from this point forward on earth?"

God was giving me the ultimate option in the exercise of my free will, and I responded immediately, "No. I'm not going to accept responsibility for the earthly life of Carl Swartz.

"I don't know what he'll do. I can't be responsible for Carl. I can't." Me play God? I couldn't.

Then God spoke with finality, "He's in My hands now."

Reverently, I spoke back, "God, if he's in Your hands, what better hands could he be in than Yours?"

Soon after, Allie and their son entered the ward and joined me at the foot of the bed; I had remained there in silence for many moments; there was no sorrow in the room.

She asked me, "What happened, Tom?"

I told her everything. Finally, I added, "He's in God's hands, Allie. Let it be."

A spiritual joy welled up in Allie, as tears spilled down her cheeks.

The son walked to his father's bedside with tears filling his eyes. With the same joyous peace of his mother, he looked at his father, paused and said, "Goodbye, dad."

At four o'clock the next morning, God took Carl to be with Him.

Allie told me, "It would have been Carl's wish, and it's our wish; we want you to preach the service at Carl's funeral."

I did. I just told the family and the friends of Carl what took place in Carl's hospital room. As the telling unfolded, it seemed, never had a roomful of people been so quiet, nor had there been such silence, such peace, such spiritual joy, such tears of love, such joyous exaltation in the grace of God, as when I told them of God's words.

I ended simply, "Aren't you pleased to leave him where he is—in God's hands?"

Everyone was.

I was, too.

20
CBN's TV Eye to the World

The center television camera adjusted position; its red light flashed on, cueing Pat Robertson where to talk to the world. "It's a pleasure to have back with us again on the 700 Club the gentleman from Oregon who made a tremendous impression when he was here before.

"He is a minister of the gospel. But about 1924 he was not a minister. He was working in a logging camp, and something happened to him. And he's going to tell us about it, so would you please welcome right now to the 700 Club Reverend Thomas Welch. (Applause)

"God bless you. Thank you for coming back. Tell me about that accident. I was so thrilled the last time I heard what God did. But others are tuned in, and maybe they haven't heard it."

It was about 10:30 Friday morning. February 16, 1979. Virginia Beach, Virginia. We were televising from the studios of the Christian Broadcasting Network (CBN).

The host of the 700 Club was Pat Robertson, president of CBN. Our program featured hell, my trip to the lake of fire and the miracle on Larch Mountain. Dr. Leslie Woodson, a theological scholar, evangelist and author from Kentucky, was also a guest on the show.

He discussed the biblical concept of hell, which he researched because he found it to be a neglected subject. Dr. Woodson felt our generation knows nothing about it, although, in his judgment, one cannot have a concept of eternal heaven without the antithesis, a concept of eternal hell.

Sitting under the hot lights in the television studio, I thought back to my first, small audience in the schoolhouse near Palmer Mill.

That was fifty-five years and three thousand miles from where I was now sitting.

And look at all this advanced communication technology.

When I responded to God that I would tell the world about the miracle on Larch Mountain, my science-fiction imagination was still working on radio, certainly not television—let alone satellites circling the globe, telecasting picture signals to earth.

What a quantum leap to this CBN program, telecast on stations throughout the United States and beamed from satellites to ground-station receivers connected to home television screens, for viewers in countries all over the world to hear what God asked be told, as they watched Pat and me in our discussion.

It was odd how personal and unnerving could be all those eyes of one hundred and twenty-five people at Palmer Mill and how impersonal and comfortable could

be the viewership of millions filtered through the un-
blinking eye of a television camera.

I had been Pat's guest once before, appearing with him
on CBN's 700 Club July 6, 1977.

When I first met Pat, I felt ill at ease in the light of his
educational accomplishments and his father having been
a distinguished United States senator from Virginia.

Pat is not unlettered; he was a Phi Beta Kappa at
Washington and Lee and has a law degree from Yale.

But, through a circuitous path in his life, he gave his
life to God and embarked on a television, radio and educational ministry.

Before long, I felt thoroughly at ease with Pat. We were
both men of God. We got on quite well on the television
programs, too.

Pat has inimitable enthusiasm and curiosity and is a
quick study. He has a rapid-fire delivery and a deep and
abiding faith.

On the 1979 program he ended his discussion with me
by appealing to all those in the television and radio audience throughout the world not to waste another minute
in a decision to escape hell by entering the kingdom of
God, "Well, there is no accounting for this except the
power of God. God raised you from the dead, and God
healed you. There's no other explanation, no way you can
give another explanation—praise God!

"You know, as this program continues, there are people
in the audience right now, and maybe you've never heard
somebody that's actually been there [to the lake of fire].

"Maybe you've just thought, oh well, I'll wait a little

while longer. But what would you do if you died tonight from an automobile accident—or something fell on you, or you had a fall, or you slipped on a ladder, or you grabbed hold of a high-powered wire, or there was an earthquake, or your heart stopped beating, or you were involved in one of the many, many, many things that can happen to somebody—and you died?

"And you went over to the other side. And there wasn't anybody there praying for you [as Mabel Brocke prayed for me], demanding, if you will, of God, that you come back into your body—and you're there forever. Just think of it—forever.

"Hell isn't for a week, and it isn't some trip to the desert where you can come back home if you don't like it.

"Hell is eternal separation from the presence of Almighty God—eternal—and those that are there know it. And they all know they could have made a different move—that's the thing.

"God doesn't do something that's unrighteous. And you've heard, if you're watching this program or listening on radio—right now, wherever you are, you've heard it.

"Now, being a church member doesn't cut it. That's nice, but that won't save you. Being a nice person won't save you.

"You must be born again. You must find Jesus if you're going to avoid 'that' place.

"I'm not talking about hell insurance. I'm talking about an exchanged life, where you're giving your life to Jesus Christ and you're serving Him as Lord and Savior.

"He is your Lord.

"Now, if you don't know Him, I'm going to let you find Him right now, so you'll know for a fact, when this program goes off the air, you're going to be saved—you're going to go to be with Jesus in heaven—and you're not going to the other place."

Pat Robertson immediately led the audience in an anointed prayer for salvation and for an infilling of the Holy Spirit.

I made my commitment to God more than half a century ago.

I don't know how many times I've told about my journey to the lake of fire and its critically relevant meaning to eternal life.

Forums have involved all forms of communication, from CBN's worldwide television to radio, books, periodicals, newspapers, churches, revivals, retreats, prayer meetings, luncheon and dinner meetings, and small groups of two or three people, even one person.

In 1978 Dr. Maurice Rawlings included a four-page report of the miracle in his book *Beyond Death's Door*.

In 1964 Gordon Lindsay published a two-page account of the miracle on Larch Mountain in his book *The Gordon Lindsay Story*. Gordon also told of our experiences together as young evangelists in Portland and El Cajon, and later through life.

In 1962, in response to innumerable requests by groups to whom I spoke, for a printed account, I finally wrote a concise report. It was printed in booklet form and included eyewitness accounts by Mabel and Fin Brocke and Julius Gunderson. Gordon Lindsay wrote the introduction, title and cover text.

This booklet, *Oregon's Amazing Miracle*, last reprinted in 1976, has had limited circulation. From the first printing I have purchased copies to distribute, without charge, to those who have heard me relate the miracle and have subsequently asked for a printed account.

The Norfolk newspaper *The Virginian-Pilot* carried a story by Ethel Steadman July 9, 1977.

On May 26, 1979, the Portland *Oregonian* featured a story by staff writer Velma Clyde, headlined, "Oregon's 'Lazarus' saw 'lake of fire.' "

In 1980 another book devoted three pages to the account of my life and death. The book is called *Life, Death and Beyond,* by J. Kerby Anderson.

The Full Gospel Business Men's Fellowship International (FGBMFI) has invited me to speak to many of their meetings. I have been delighted to do so. I have long been impressed with the ministry of the founder and president of FGBMFI, Demos Shakarian, a dynamic and unassuming man of God, truly filled with the Holy Spirit, and an eminently successful businessman.

I have been approached several times to enter into promotional schemes. As soon as I learned the true nature of the proposals, I have refused to have anything to do with them.

I have been convinced from the very beginning it would be an abomination and an affront to God should I knowingly allow any profiteering from the miracle.

Moreover, in this matter I must speak with candor. My faith in God so transcends this world that when I lay hands on any person, I do not want any taint of profiteering to interfere with the beautiful flow of the love and power of Jesus Christ.

I have poured all my energy and resources into fulfilling my commitment to God. And I shall continue to do so.

However, in my humble judgment, it matters not that millions of people may have heard the meaning of the miracle on Larch Mountain.

It matters only the number of those who have listened, hearkened and stepped forward to enter the kingdom of God.

As Pat Robertson said, "Hell isn't for a week, and it isn't some trip to the desert where you can come back home if you don't like it.

"Hell is eternal separation from the presence of Almighty God—eternal . . ."

Looking to the years ahead, all but one portion of the prophecy given to us by God in 1926 has been fulfilled.

Many years ago I was startled to discover the striking similarity of the final episode of a vision seen by General George Washington at Valley Forge and the final portion of the prophetic words given to us in El Cajon, both foretelling a worldly event yet to unfold.

21
Unfulfilled Prophetic Words

General George Washington had a vision in 1777 while seated alone in his command tent at Valley Forge.

He later told an associate of the event and what he saw revealed to him.

The final portion of his vision, as interpreted by Dr. Charles R. Taylor in his book *World War III and the Destiny of America,* parallels the only unfulfilled chapter of the divine prophecy unveiled to Peterson, Lindsay, Hall and me in El Cajon, California, in 1926.

At the time, the prophecy puzzled us; we were stunned by the revelation of momentous events, yet each of those events, with one exception, has unfolded.

The Great Depression became the time of widespread famine, poverty, suffering, hunger and starvation.

World War II became the arena in which great nations of the world collided, with unbelievable destruction, bloodshed and death, over a period of many years.

The third and fourth episodes of the prophecy do not lend themselves to beautifully ribboned packaging.

There has been an ebb and flow in the gifts of the Spirit. Right after World War II there seemed to be a low-water mark, until the late 1940s.

From then until late in the 1950s there was an outpouring of the gifts of the Spirit, especially healing, through churches and increasingly through lay people. This was a period of restoration.

For the next twenty years, until just before the 1980s, no portion of the prophecy has been regrettably more accurate insofar as mass abandonment of God. Affluence has been rampant and has spawned a helter-skelter pursuit of money and power and the reckless gratification of esteem, self, sexual appetites and all the pleasures of the senses.

Unbelief has swept the earth, and sadly it has become true, "They that believe, will believe no more." The gifts of the Spirit waned during this period.

However, another restoration began before the turn of the 1980s, one that will dwarf the 1950s and will spread like a tidal wave through lay people all over the world.

This renaissance will sweep the North American continent until it is shattered by the mushrooming war clouds of the final chapter of the prophetic words at El Cajon.

It was not until many years later, after El Cajon, that I learned of a vision which appeared before General Washington at Valley Forge.

In his book, Dr. Charles Taylor relates a meeting between publisher Wesley Bradshaw and Anthony Sherman, who was a colleague of General Washington and who was with him at Valley Forge.

Sherman disclosed what General Washington had told him. The content of the vision was published in *The National Tribune* in December, 1880, and again in *The Stars and Stripes* December 21, 1950.

General Washington was in his command tent alone when a mysterious, airy, beautiful being appeared before him. Visions of scenes began to appear, and a voice spoke to him.

The visions have been interpreted to be of the Revolutionary War then in progress, the Civil War, the development of the United States as a nation, World War III and the destiny of the United States.

Because of striking similarities between General Washington's vision and God's prophetic words to us in 1926, it is interesting to examine the final portion of the vision, which Dr. Taylor interprets as foretelling World War III and the destiny of the United States.

As General Washington related the final episode, "Again I heard the mysterious voice saying, 'Son of the Republic, look and learn.' At this the dark, shadowy angel placed a trumpet to his mouth, and blew three distinct blasts; and taking water from the ocean, he sprinkled it upon Europe, Asia and Africa.

"Then my eyes beheld a fearful scene. From each of these continents arose thick black clouds that were soon joined into one. And through this mass there gleamed a dark red light by which I saw hordes of armed men.

"These men, moving with the cloud, marched by land and sailed by sea to America, which country was enveloped in the volume of the cloud.

143

"And I dimly saw these vast armies devastate the whole country and burn the villages, towns and cities which I had seen springing up.

"As my ears listened to the thundering of the cannon, clashing of swords, and the shouts and cries of millions in mortal combat, I again heard the mysterious voice saying, 'Son of the Republic, look and learn.'

"When this voice had ceased, the dark shadowy angel placed his trumpet once more to his mouth, and blew a long and fearful blast.

"Instantly a light as of a thousand suns shone down from above me, and pierced and broke into fragments the dark cloud which enveloped America.

"At the same moment the angel upon whose head still shown the word 'Union' and who bore our national flag in one hand, a sword in the other, descended from the heavens attended by legions of white spirits.

"These immediately joined the inhabitants of America, who I perceived were well-nigh overcome, but who immediately taking courage again, closed up their broken ranks and renewed the battle.

"Again, amid the fearful noise of the conflict I heard the mysterious voice saying, 'Son of the Republic, look and learn.'

"As the voice ceased, the shadowy angel for the last time dipped water from the ocean and sprinkled it upon America. Instantly the dark cloud rolled back, together with the armies it had brought, leaving the inhabitants of the land victorious.

"Then once more, I beheld the villages, towns and cities

springing up where I had seen them before, while the bright angel, planting the azure standard he had brought in the midst of them, cried with a loud voice, 'While the stars remain, and the heavens send down dew upon the earth, so long shall the union last.'

"And taking from his brow the crown on which blazoned the word 'Union' he placed it upon the standard while the people kneeling down said, 'Amen.'

"The scene instantly began to fade and dissolve, and I at last saw nothing but the rising, curling vapor I at first beheld. This also disappeared, and I found myself once more gazing upon the mysterious visitor, who, in the same voice I had heard before, said, 'Son of the Republic, what you have seen is thus interpreted.

" 'Three great perils will come upon the Republic. The most fearful for her is the third.

" 'But the whole world united shall not prevail against her. Let every child of the Republic learn to live for his God, his land and union!'

"With these words the vision vanished, and I started from my seat and felt that I had seen a vision wherein had been shown me the birth, the progress, and the destiny of the United States."

As in General Washington's vision, one chapter of the prophetic words to us in El Cajon in 1926 also belongs to the future.

The likeness is incredible.

God told us there will be another great war, visiting upon the earth the most violent holocaust the world has ever seen.

The world will be divided into two warring camps, those of God in one and the godless in the other.

Death, disease, hunger, starvation, sickness, confusion, destruction and suffering will cover the earth on a scale never before seen.

One-third of the population of the world shall perish.

God then told us that from the ashes the North American civilization shall rise to unassailable power, and on that continent there will be a rebirth of spiritual and intellectual holiness which will lead the world to greater wisdom, understanding, knowledge and love in God.

Therein is the power—in God's love, in the Holy Spirit.

God told us in this time He will pour out and spread His Spirit throughout His people.

22

Why Me, a Miracle?

Why me, a miracle?

When I was young, oh, how easily I could have answered that question. But now I know too much; what I really mean, now I know there is so much I don't know.

I have pondered that question many times.

I have put it on the floor in my mind and walked around it, and examined it, and looked at it from every perspective on the compass.

What happened to me has happened to others, both men and women.

Some people living today, and I'm sure in the past, have been with the Lord, either during their lives or in circumstances similar to mine, where the door of death has been left ajar, for some of us to return, and a few of us to be sent back by the Lord himself.

Undoubtedly others have seen the lake of fire. The Apostle John saw it according to the Holy Scripture:

And I saw a great white throne, and him that sat on it, from whose face the earth and the heaven fled away; and there was found no place for them.

And I saw the dead, small and great, stand before God; and the books were opened: and another book was opened, which is the book of life: and the dead were judged out of those things which were written in the books, according to their works.

And the sea gave up the dead which were in it; and death and hell delivered up the dead which were in them; and they were judged every man according to their works.

And death and hell were cast into the lake of fire. This is the second death.

And whosoever was not found written in the book of life was cast into the lake of fire. (Rev. 20:11-15)

Martin Luther and others have been confronted by Satan in experiences similar to mine. In fact, it is well known Luther threw an inkwell at Satan. The spot where the well struck a wall in his office in Wittenberg, Germany, remains preserved today.

Why I came to witness the lake of fire rather than heaven or some other sphere in eternity, I don't know.

It's true, at eighteen I was bitter about my lot in life and still angry at God for being orphaned into the world at eleven. I've asked myself: in the eyes of God, was I that rebellious? Was I a heathen? Was I an infidel? Did I commit such magnitude of sin by shaking my fist in the face of God, I was sent to hell to see the awesome horror of the ocean of fire, the place of eternal separation from Almighty God? I will have to leave that to God, and to you. I am at peace.

The miracle on Larch Mountain is inseparable from the tapestry of my entire life.

If I had chosen a path different from the one I walked, it could have been otherwise. But I have lived my life according to the commitment I made to God in my bed at Good Samaritan Hospital.

The miracle has enriched the meaning of my ministry, and my ministry has enriched the meaning of the miracle.

Each of us will stand before God in the final Great White Throne Judgment. I don't subscribe to the concept that God is a big, jolly, white-haired grandfather upon whose knee we'll sit and get a pat on the head no matter what we've been doing.

Each of us will be held accountable before God according to the Holy Scriptures. How we choose to live on earth will be weighed by God in His judgment of our eternity.

It grieves me to see people living as if there's no tomorrow. Tomorrow is eternity.

Eternity can be joyous. Or eternity can be a final death, forever.

I have been to the lake of fire. I have seen it. I know those who are found wanting before the Great White Throne shall perish in that lake. I can tell you there is life after death, and there is death after death.

When I was a guest of Pat Robertson on the 700 Club television program of the Christian Broadcasting Network in 1979, Dr. Woodson, another guest, and I privately discussed my role in the miracle and particularly, why did God want my eyewitness account of the lake of fire told on earth during this century?

Dr. Woodson told me his judgment; God in His foreknowledge knows the purpose of my testimony in that He knows the plan He foreordained from time immemorial, and the miracle has become woven into that plan, which coincides with its revelation at this time.

Dr. Woodson correlated the meaning of what the Bible says about the lake of fire with the freedom of choice facing mankind today. He emphasized that after the final judgment by God, all false religions, false beliefs, the antichrists and the abominable, along with those people who rejected Jesus Christ, will be cast into the lake of fire. I agree with Dr. Woodson.

It matters not, in my opinion, *where* mankind becomes aware of what is foreordained, whether it is learned from the Holy Scriptures or through God's miracle on Larch Mountain. It matters only that mankind is forewarned.

Over time, I have examined the meaning of the resurrection of Lazarus, to gain insight why the lake of fire did not appear to me in a vision or in some other way. Why was my death so violent? Why was a miracle involved at all?

Why was I chosen to die, see the lake of fire, be sent back to life by Jesus and be asked to tell the world what I saw and how I came back to life?

The Lord himself knew, illustrated by what He said just before he raised Lazarus from the dead. Jesus spoke to Martha, sister of Lazarus:

> Jesus saith unto her, Said I not unto thee, that, if thou wouldest believe, thou shouldest see the glory of God?

> Then they took away the stone from the place where the dead was laid. And Jesus lifted up his eyes, and said, Father, I thank thee that thou hast heard me.

> And I knew that thou hearest me always: but because of the people which stand by I said it, that they may believe that thou hast sent me.

> And when he thus had spoken, he cried with a loud voice, Lazarus, come forth.

> And he that was dead came forth, bound hand and foot with graveclothes: and his face was bound about with a napkin. Jesus saith unto them, Loose him, and let him go. (John 11:40-44)

That's why I believe a miracle of my resurrection was involved and that the Lord asked me specifically not only to tell the world what I saw, but also *how I came back to life*; Jesus wanted the world to know, as He did at the resurrection of Lazarus, this was a miracle of God: "because of the people which stand by I said it, that they may believe that thou hast sent me." Thus, can the meaning of the miracle on Larch Mountain be ignored?

Introspection has, at times, focused on my bulldog tenacity to remain with my ministry after I told the Lord,

"Yes," from my hospital bed at such an early age, and I have always come up with the same answer. God knew me, of course, better than I knew myself.

He knew that if I answered His question affirmatively, I would be faithful. I have been faithful in my life and in my commitment to Him.

God knows, too, in one sense, how excruciating it has been to tell what I saw. The reality of the lake of fire is as vivid right now as if I've just returned.

I shall never in my life be able to tell about my visit without reliving the experience. After telling about it for more than half a century, one might think everything would become callously routine, with no aftereffects.

I have related my story countless times, and every time I do, my hairs stand on end with a supernatural tingling, identical to the spine-chilling sensation I felt when I was standing on the shoreline of the lake of fire.

And every time afterward, I have retreated into the night, unable to sleep, immensely disturbed for mankind, wracked in pain, with my soul tortured by the presence of the cataclysmic terror of that final inferno.

However, in another sense, I share my joy with God each time I relate the miracle.

It's easy to talk about and describe something I've seen. I know there is a lake of fire because I have seen it. I know Jesus Christ is alive in eternity. I have seen Him there.

I feel deeply, spiritually privileged to have been chosen to help point the way for mankind to eternal life.

And I shall continue to tell the world what I've seen, and how I came back to life.

Perhaps the most eloquent answer to all the questions surrounding the miracle on Larch Mountain was the response to Mabel Brocke, when she was startled to be told I had fallen off the trestle to my death. Mabel protested, completely dismayed, "Why Tommy?"

And she heard the voice of the Holy Spirit tell her, "For the glory of God."

"What's Past Is Prologue"

God has a purpose for the miracle on Larch Mountain.

God has a purpose in asking me to relate the miracle to you. I won't presume to speculate on that significance. I'll respectfully leave that to God and to you.

However, if you would permit me, I do have a perspective on a meaning of the miracle. Christians, emerging Christians, theologians, scholars and others are welcome to shade configurations they may see.

Nonetheless, I do wish humbly to craft a hub of confluence into which all the tributaries, of which you are now aware, seem to flow.

At the epicenter of the confluence are two questions. One final. The other, preliminary.

The final question is this: how do we wish to spend eternity?

The choice is simply: eternal life or eternal death. Eternal life with Almighty God. Or, eternal separation from Almighty God.

It's not a meaningless, frivolous decision.

We must make the decision.

We can't muddle through. We'll make the choice one way or the other. By not choosing, we choose.

The miracle on Larch Mountain is a joyous triumph of the *living,* not the dead. *Eternal life,* not eternal death.

Jesus raised me from the dead to the *living.*

God is the God of the *living,* not the dead, as Jesus has told us.

I was chosen to die, journey to the next world to witness the reality of the lake of fire and return to *life,* so that we may be forewarned and choose a path of *eternal life.*

The preliminary question is this: how do we wish to spend our time on earth?

Of the awesome power of our own free will, God's gift to each of us, Jesus issued the ultimate, solemn warning for mankind, in my hospital room at Good Samaritan: "a man may choose a righteous or evil path, and verily I say unto you: upon the earthly path of your feet, God will render a final judgment for the eternal path of your soul."

It's a personal choice.

Whatever time you have left on earth—one hundred minutes or one hundred years—if you have not made your personal choice, I prayerfully entreat you to enter the kingdom of God, right now, be born of the Holy Spirit of Jesus Christ and choose to walk a righteous path in this world, so that you will abide in eternal life with Almighty God.

Our Supplication Together for You

If you've never made the choice, it would be my earnest hope and prayer you will make it right now. Could this be your last chance? For some, it may. Make your choice now, and settle forever in your own heart and mind the path you will walk during the remainder of your lifetime—and the eternal path of your soul.

One day I expect to see you in the everlasting presence of God, if you will bow your head right now and dedicate yourself to embody and reflect, from this moment on, the honor and glory and Holy Spirit of the Lord Jesus Christ.

Simply bow your head in prayer and say the following words of our supplication together for you, so that you may enter the kingdom of God and be born again in the Holy Spirit—at this very moment:

Lord God, Your Holy Word tells us if we say we have no sin we deceive ourselves and the truth is not in us, but if we confess our sins, You are faithful and just to forgive us and to cleanse us from all unrighteousness.

Lord Jesus, to this moment I have lived my life for me, without you. Lord, I am a sinner; I have sinned. Lord, I don't want to go to hell. I want to be with You forever in heaven. Jesus, I confess and repent of my sins.

I turn away from unrighteousness, Jesus, and receive You as Lord of my life. Come into my life, Lord Jesus. Live Your life in me and I will serve You all the days of my life.

Thank you, Jesus, that You have heard my confession, my repentance and my prayer and You have forgiven me and cleansed me of all my sins and have now, at this moment, come into my heart to dwell in my new life. Amen.

And now, I, Reverend Welch, offer reverent supplication that this new Christian in Christ be born again of the Spirit:

Lord, You have said, "That which is born of the flesh is flesh; and that which is born of the Spirit is spirit." Further, "Verily, verily, I say unto thee, Except a man be born of water and of the Spirit, he cannot enter into the kingdom of God." Further, "Marvel not that I said unto thee, Ye must be born again."

Father, for this new Christian who has just prayed with me to You, may the anointing power of the Holy Spirit touch this Christian now, in Your name, in the name of Jesus. My Christian friend, be filled with the Holy Spirit, be filled with His power, now, at this moment, in Jesus' name. Amen. And Amen.

God bless you, my Christian friend, in your new life.

Rev. Thomas Welch

Appendix 1

Eyewitness Julius H. Gunderson

He prepared this statement for the booklet Oregon's Amazing Miracle, *first published in 1962 by Christ For The Nations, Inc., Dallas, Texas. Reprinted by permission.*

I, J.H. Gunderson, was at the Palmer Mill looking for a job and visiting Fin Brocke on June 30, 1924, when at about one-thirty in the afternoon Tom fell and I witnessed this miracle of faith.

A locomotive engineer sitting in his cab saw Tom fall. He ran from his locomotive down into the main engine room to tell Mr. Brocke what had happened.

The mill was shut down and Mr. Brocke and I and others went to recover Tom, but he had fallen into the water, which was ten feet deep at this point. We had a hard time finding him because the water was dirty and we were fishing for him with pike poles with long handles. After some time, another man gave me the pole he was using and I began probing the water deep down because I felt that he must be on the bottom.

This was right because after some time of this kind of searching I hooked onto his clothes and pulled his body near enough for us to get our hands on him, and we pulled him out. He was dead. There was no life in him at all. His head was smashed in on top and blood was everywhere.

Mrs. Brocke got word and came down to the mill. When she saw Tom lying there still and dead, she knelt down and put her hand on his head. The blood oozed out between her fingers as she cried out to God to spare his life and save his soul because Tom was not a Christian.

As she cried out and prayed, I saw life come back into Tom and he moved for the first time since we had recovered him from the water. Then he opened his eyes and asked, "What happened?"

Over these years I have thanked God many times for the privilege I had of seeing a dead man come back to life in answer to prayer. I stood on the bank of that pond for at least thirty minutes while other men were fishing for his body. I was watching for air bubbles or some sign of where he was. I never did see any air bubbles. There was no water in his lungs. He never had breathed in all that time he was under the water.

One of the men who had been trying to find Tom had given up and handed me his pike pole. I pushed it down deep and it hooked onto his clothing. He must have been near the bottom. It must have been all of forty-five minutes to one hour from the time he fell until Mrs. Brocke prayed for him in the mill office.

This is my testimony as I saw it happen. I pulled Tom to the surface myself, and witnessed the miracle of life restored in him. I thank God for what I saw that day, and I thank God for the privilege of telling it here. It changed my life. It is the truth.

Julius H. Gunderson

Appendix 2

Eyewitness Mabel Brocke (countersigned by her husband)

This statement was prepared for the booklet Oregon's Amazing Miracle, *first published in 1962 by Christ For The Nations, Inc., Dallas, Texas. Reprinted by permission.*

I had gone over the hillside to pick some berries, but the rain had chased me in. I was within a few yards of our house when I saw my husband coming, walking fast, and he called to me and said, "Mama, Tommy fell and he is dead."

It is just as fresh in my memory now as then, what I said and how I felt. I asked, "Why Tommy?" and I heard a voice say, "For the Glory of God." Then my husband said, "I came to get you to pray."

I went with him back to the mill office. We didn't talk but we did pray all the way. When we got back to the office the room was filled with men and there lay Tommy wrapped in a blanket on a table. His face and head were covered with blood; there was no pulse, no life. Surely we were in the presence of death. You could feel it, as well as see it.

Those men that were packed in there knew my husband. They knew he was a man of prayer, and that he had gone to get me to help him pray. They were expecting to see something happen. I went to one side of the table and my husband went to the other side.

The Bible says in James 5:14 and 15: "Is any sick among you? let him call for the elders of the church; and let them pray over him, anointing him with oil in the name of the Lord: And the prayer of faith shall save the sick, and the Lord shall raise him up; and if he have committed sins, they shall be forgiven him."

My husband anointed him with oil according to the Scripture, and then he said, "Mabel, you pray." I placed one hand on his head and the other on his heart. A young man standing near took my hand off Tommy's head and said, "Can't you see that is where he is hurt?" It wasn't a long prayer. We just asked God to be merciful and raise him up.

First we saw his eyelids move just a little; then the tears began to come and he tried to talk. He said, "What happened?" The words were far apart, as though they were coming from a far country. Then he said, "I can't help it now."

More life came into him and the men standing around were all amazed and happy. They had seen a miracle. The boss had called Portland for an ambulance soon after Tommy fell, and we knew it would be coming soon.

When they got him to the hospital, he was taken into surgery and they cleaned the wounds in his head and put a lot of stitches in his scalp. Seven ribs on his left side were broken; they bandaged him up for that. It took a long time to do all this and we waited until they brought him out of surgery. He didn't say anything so we asked him if he had any pain. He said, "No."

They took him to the intensive care ward, and then he asked the nurse if he could have something to eat. They did give him something to eat before we left him to go back to the mill. My husband was the chief engineer so we had to go back that night.

I returned to the hospital the next morning. The doctors asked me not to stay long; they did not hold out much hope that he would live. It was hard for Tommy to talk and his words came very slowly.

He said, "I have something to tell you. You know I was dead for a while, but I found myself way off in a wilderness. It was as if a huge magnet were drawing me into it, and a lot of other people too, and there was no way to get out. I saw my uncle and a boy I went to school with. There was a great big lake of fire and I felt as if I were being drawn into it. I was afraid.

"Then I saw Jesus coming from a way off. He came closer and was going on by, and I said, 'If He would only turn and look at me He would save me.' Then Jesus looked at me and I heard you praying. I opened my eyes as soon as I could and I saw you."

I had to leave then, but later on he told us about all the things he had seen. He talked a lot about the lake of fire and the ones there. He said there was not anybody in the fire, but they were in a prison waiting and there was no way to escape.

The next time we saw Tommy was on a Friday night, after work. We did not know about what had taken place in the hospital that morning. When we got to my sister's home in Portland, we found that he was no longer in the hospital and that he had been instantly healed and had left the hospital about eleven o'clock that morning.

He was in the hospital just four days. He went back to the mill with us that night and was back to work on Saturday.

Sunday night he told his experience at the little schoolhouse near the mill. The entire mill crew and their families were there. Many could not get inside the building; it was too small.

They had seen a miracle. Now they wanted to hear about it. Needless to say, we were very grateful to God for letting us have a part in this great thing that He had done. Tommy has kept his word and has been telling his story and preaching faith and deliverance ever since. Have faith in God. He never fails when we believe.

Mabel Brocke
Thorfin Brocke

Appendix 3

Testimony by Gordon Lindsay

Introduction by Gordon Lindsay to the booklet Oregon's
Amazing Miracle, *first published in 1962 by Christ For
The Nations, Inc., Dallas, Texas. Reprinted by permission.*

I have known Thomas Welch the greater part of his
life. In fact, I met him shortly after the amazing miracle
in which he was brought back to life after being dead
nearly an hour. To some people Tom's testimony will
seem incredible, but the documentation of it is absolute.

After the engineer who was operating the yard engine
had witnessed Tom's 55-foot fall, he at once sounded the
alarm. The large mill was immediately shut down and
perhaps 75 men participated in the attempt to locate the
body, which was lying somewhere in the murky waters of
the pond. Nearly an hour passed before they located the
body and pulled it out and laid it lifeless in the mill office.

They witnessed Mrs. Brocke's compassionate prayer
and cry to God for Him to bring Tom back to life, and
following the prayer, saw the flickering of his eyelids.

Still more astonished were the men at the mill when they saw him back on the job Saturday, just six days later.

Then on the following Sunday night they heard him relate his fantastic story in the little schoolhouse (where I, too, later preached). Not less amazing was the instantaneous miracle in the hospital on Friday when each broken bone instantly came into place.

As Tom testifies, he had become an infidel early in his life from reading books in his uncle's library which included the works of Voltaire, Thomas Paine and Robert G. Ingersoll.

His experience in the nether world instantly showed him the falsity of the philosophies of these notorious advocates of agnosticism and infidelity. In the brief time Tom spent there, he saw that the spirit of man exists after death of the body and he that rejects Christ must spend eternity elsewhere than with Him.

Not long after this experience I was converted in the same church, one pastored by Dr. John G. Lake, in Portland. Tom kept his promise that he made to the Lord on the hospital bed when he was miraculously healed. A year later he and I and L.D. Hall left Portland to begin preaching the Gospel.

Bibliography

Anderson, J. Kerby. *Life, Death and Beyond*. Grand Rapids, Mich.: Zondervan, 1980.

Buckingham, Jamie. *Daughter of Destiny: Kathryn Kuhlman*. Plainfield, N.J.: Logos International, 1976.

Kerns, Phil and Doug Wead. *People's Temple—People's Tomb*. Plainfield, N.J.: Logos International, 1979.

Lindsay, Gordon. *The Gordon Lindsay Story*. Dallas, Texas: The Voice of Healing Publishing Co., 1964.

Lindsay, Gordon. *Prayer That Moves Mountains*. Dallas, Texas: Christ For The Nations, 1979.

Lindsay, Gordon, editor. *The John G. Lake Sermons*. Dallas, Texas: Christ For The Nations, reprinted, 1978.

Rawlings, Maurice, M.D. *Beyond Death's Door*. Nashville, New York: Thomas Nelson, Inc., 1978.

Robertson, Pat and Jamie Buckingham. *Shout It From the Housetops*. Plainfield, N.J.: Logos International, 1972.

Taylor, Charles R., Ph.D. *World War III and the Destiny of America*. Nashville, Tenn.: Thomas Nelson, Inc., 1979.

Welch, Thomas H. *Oregon's Amazing Miracle*. Dallas, Texas: The Voice of Healing Publishing Co., 1962. Reprinted, under same publisher's new name, Christ For The Nations, 1976.